JADA MONICA DREW

More Than Enough
STEP INTO THE NEXT LEVEL OF YOU

SOCIAL DESIGNS

MORE THAN ENOUGH
Copyright © 2017 by Jada Monica Drew
All rights reserved.

Printed Book- ISBN: 978-0-9974333-2-6
Electronic Book- ISBN: 978-0-9974333-3-3

Book design by KPE Media

Published and printed in the United States by Social Designs
www.socialdesignsconsulting.com

First Edition

*For my talented, beautiful, loving,
and courageous nieces;*

Whitney Arjeudi

Paris Ann

Megan Elizabeth

Tyler Carla

Morgan Nicole

Bailee Rae

Nakyah Rene

Contents

From Jada, with Love 7

More Than Enough Terminology 12

Introduction 15

Steps to the Next Level of You

STEP ONE: ASK YOURSELF WHY 21
    Dismiss the potential
    Own your own power
    Satisfy a need

STEP TWO: REFLECT DEEPLY 31
    Take a time out
    Practice mindfulness
    Conquer the inconsistencies
    Seek knowledge

STEP THREE: DETOX 45
    Practice purity
    Bounce back from "outages"
    Let go

STEP FOUR: START A JOURNEY
OF RESEARCH 57
    Develop an inquisitive mindset
    Plant the seeds
    Don't be afraid to ask for help

STEP FIVE: TRUST THE
EXPIRATION DATE 69

    Put a date on everything
    Don't ignore the signs
    Build your capacity to keep going
    Sharpen your BS meter

STEP SIX: UNPLUG 83
    Get in sync
    Explore nature
    Mind your business

STEP SEVEN: JUST DO IT NOW 95
    Celebrate the genius in you
    Create an idea-nation
    Chew on your mistakes

STEP EIGHT: COMPETE WITH
YOUR YESTERDAY 111
    Create your own lane
    Filter the feedback
    Work smarter and harder
    Lead with boldness

STEP NINE: THRIVE 123
    Find joy
    Stay in the lab
    Practice discipline
    Reinvent yourself

Closing 137
References 139
Glossary 140
Jada's Motivation Playlist 141
Acknowledgements 143

From Jada, with Love

Being vulnerable, honest, and believing in a better world are so essential in people-centered professions like mine. It is a constant act for me to acknowledge insecurities and to be confident each day. I'm truly happy and thriving because I'm constantly searching for and finding the balance of merging authenticity with brutal truths. This is my bittersweet spot. I bask in bitter lies about myself if they make me feel good or if I'm receiving immediate incentives for unhealthy behavior. Yet, when these lies are uncovered and new habits are realized the reward is much sweeter.

Journey with me to a place of constant thriving where your joy and your celebrations outweigh your sorrows and challenges. Step into the *next level* of you, not because you want to, but because merely existing is not enough. Think of thriving and being *more than enough* as mandatory obligations in your life. Love on yourself and your talents, but also love on your weaknesses long enough to witness them and change for the better. Being *more than enough* means that you have developed the habits needed to unpack the baggage that has been placed in your psyche and heart telling you that you are not enough. But to be very clear, you are *More Than Enough*. You are more than your failures. You are more than your insecurities. You have the responsibility to think outside the box and to envision a better, more refined and more courageous version of yourself.

Believe and behave in your boldness. This may disturb the comfortable and push people to their growing edge, but so what? Don't be afraid to make a little noise to spark a *lot* of change. Being bold means loving yourself despite your shortcomings, but loving yourself enough to change and to accept that you need to transform. When you reframe your thinking, you re-develop yourself into a more intentional human being. The mistakes don't stop, you are just more aware of yourself and the impact of those mistakes.

Most people fail to realize the ripple effect of their positive or negative impact. I encourage you to stay with yourself long enough to study the effect you have on yourself and the effect you have on others. Be mindful and discover those things about your personality that you want to keep and those things you want to let go. On your journey to constantly being *More Than Enough*, share affirmations and encouragement to those around you.

Affirmations to my nieces …

In a world of uncertainties, *you* are a constant. All of you bring joy to me in your own unique way. You will continue to offer so much to the world, and that's a fact. While you are offering your gifts of joy, kindness and brilliance to the world, make sure you save some of that goodness for yourself and don't steer away from your magic. Always know that who you are today and who you are becoming tomorrow is *More Than Enough*.

Whitney Arjeudi, the way your crafty hands and creative do-it-yourself home projects evolve make me smile. Your drive and constant connection to home and tradition fills my spirit.

With the rosiest smile I've ever seen, *Paris Ann*, you will always be the first baby I heard call me auntie and at 26, you still have the sweetest voice and the most giving heart that shines so bright.

Megan Elizabeth, the world traveler who is down to earth and relatable enough to blend in every culture and country you've lived in. Your boldness to be courageous encourages me.

You have the most contagious and joyous laugh I've ever heard. *Tyler Carla*, from when you were a little girl to now as a grown woman, your realness encourages others to be truthful and solid. You are our family's rock and connector for the next generation.

Morgan Nicole, my goof troop number two. When you perform, the world stops and listens to your spirit. Don't dim that light, because many of us need it to keep going.

Bailee Rae, the sweetest heart of all. Your soul is sensitive to others because you have a keen internal connection to everyone you meet. If you never say anything, your presence requires everyone to listen.

When you enter a room *Nakyah Rene*, everyone must stop and pay attention. Your bubbly personality and great attention to detail makes each person you encounter feel loved, appreciated, and happy.

Each of you are ***More Than Enough***!
Love,
Auntie Jada

Let someone in your life know that they are *More Than Enough*. Make a list of three people and provide an example of how each is *More Than Enough*. Think of a creative way to share this with each of them.

_____
_____
_____
_____
_____
_____
_____
_____
_____
_____
_____
_____
_____
_____
_____
_____
_____

Revolutionize Now Terminology

More Than Enough is written in standardized United States English, African American Vernacular English, and regional slang. In the process of writing, it has been important for me to proudly acknowledge my language as a tool of celebration. I celebrate linguistic variety while writing, presenting, and teaching. Throughout this book you will experience and learn from my culture through language. An explanation of terms that are '_____' can be found below.

9-5 - a regular job with an 8-hour work day

A Different World - a sitcom of the 1990s that was a comical yet poignant look at student life at Hillman College, a fictional historically Black college, by a diverse group of students who discover the joys and trials of adulthood.

And Roses - a social justice beach house

Baggage - past experiences or long-held ideas regarded as burdens and impediments

Black Wallstreet - prominent communities around the United States where Black people owned businesses, and held political power.

BS- bull s**t - nonsense, lies, or exaggeration

By the skin of your teeth - just barely accomplishing a goal or task

Check - to put someone in their place; to realize your current situation

Chill - to calm down, to hang out

Clutter-bug - one who excessively accumulates junk or clutter

Conscious - being in a state of awareness, understanding intersections of identity and social systems from historical and contemporary perspectives

Cultural cues - a thing said or done that serves as a signal for someone to behave according to the accepted culture of an environment

Cry over spilled milk - complain, and sulk in one's mistakes. To remain upset about a past loss.

Cut up - to have a fabulous time

Dirty laundry - private business that is usually embarrassing

Don't believe in fire, until fire burns - one fails to believe others until they experience something themselves

Don't throw the baby out with the bath water - an idiomatic expression for an avoidable error in which something good is eliminated when trying to get rid of something bad, or in other words, rejecting the essential along with the inessential.

Ducks in a row - complete composure; to make sure things are running smoothly

Grit - a mindset of courage, passion and perseverance towards reaching a short and long-term goal

Hard-headed - A person who once they have their mind set on something it isn't easily changed

Humble beginnings - low financial material and financial assets early on in life or after a period of severe loss

Hungry - extremely eager and overzealous to achieve a goal

Keep it pushing - to continue to move forward even when obstacles are in the way

Lurking - spying on people online, while you remain invisible.

Nit-picking - looking for small or unimportant errors or faults, especially to criticize unnecessarily

No-brainer - something that requires or involves little or no mental effort

Out and about - being out of one's living quarters and traveling around an area

Peopling - socializing

Reaping what you sow - you will harvest that which you plant. Figuratively it means that you will obtain consequences in accord with the actions you take, or not.

Proof in the pudding - evidence is in the action or the result

Savage - someone who does not care about consequences related to their actions

Slay - to dominate, doing something of great skill

Spanglish - a combination of the Spanish and English languages

Sugarcoat - to make the truth sound less harsh; telling half-truths; beating around the bush

Staying the course - continue to do something until its finished

Tail end - the very end

Tending to - paying attention to a task, a person, or a project

Thrivers - people who seek to live their happiest and at the height of personal success

Twice as hard - the necessity to need to over-work, over-produce, and over-achieve as a strategy to avoid as much discrimination as possible based on marginalized identities

Vibe - A distinctive emotional atmosphere; sensed intuitively

We are all a work in progress - the path to growth while working hard towards goals

Woke - to be conscious about systems of oppression and empowerment movements

Introduction

Reflections in Topsail Beach, North Carolina

This morning I woke up with feelings of gratitude. There was a sense of calm over my body because of the rumbling of the waves and the stillness of the sky. My heartbeat was steady and my eyes wide awake as my body was eager to get down to the ocean. The level of calmness increased because of my daily routine of praying and drinking a glass of water. While walking to the beach, I observed every detail. The two-lane highway with specks of miniature gravel and concrete with a faint paired yellow line down the middle of the road. I walked under a wooden-arched entrance leading me to stairs reading "private entrance." Stepping slow and steady down 30 stairs, I drew closer to the squeaky and recently dew-dampened sand. As I spotted the perfect area of sand for my beach blanket, I smiled at the man fishing with his daughter in the near distance. It reminded me of my grandfather's and mother's shared love for fishing and my daddy's love for me.

My focus was on having a serene yoga session in the perfect 68-degree weather, fueled by my desire to get closer to me and closer to a higher power. Beach goers passed by with the same look in their eyes; a need for early morning serenity.

With my timer set for 10 minutes, I proceeded with yoga positions starting with Downward Facing Dog, Warrior, The Tree, and Bridge poses in the sand. At first, I was an awkward sight to see while seeking balance on the uneven beach. Once I found balance and I became a beautiful and peaceful vision. I was encapsulated in my Zen. When my yoga session ended, a strong energy pulling from the waves begged me to stay just a little bit longer. Sitting on a vibrant cobalt blue, hot pink, and sunset yellow fabric I crossed my legs in a peaceful position of surrender.

Closing my eyes, I breathed deeply.
> Moments in time flashed through my mind…
> Of when I was afraid to let go
> When the fear of breathing deeply was too much to take.
> When the anxiety of the unknown plagued my bloodstream
> When I did not believe I was good enough to have all my heart desired.
> When I did not have the courage to speak with extreme confidence
> When I entered and stayed in friendships and relationships that were toxic.

Closing my eyes, I breathed deeply again.
> I decided that I was *More Than Enough*.
> The reality of my genius and power of my dignity filled my spirit.
> The personality and presence I was blessed with excited me more.
> Courageously, I stepped into unknown territory.

Closing my eyes, I breathed deeply and smiled knowing that I am *More Than Enough*.

Two years ago, I would have never imagined that I would be retreating on the beach at 'And Roses' having this life changing epiphany. These and many other blessings have continued show me the possibilities of God. Not only was I blessed with the time to reflect and breathe but I was also able to do that with friends who have values of justice and peace. In gratitude, my life will never be the same.

Do you ever get that feeling of knowing there is something you long to do, a place you desire to go, or a person with whom you want to connect? This gut feeling presents an opportunity to try something new. It may even push you to speak up with more conviction. What about that feeling when you know your future is out there for you to accomplish and conquer anything and everything, yet you are immobile and paralyzed by your own fears? Have you ever chosen not to do anything because you do not believe in yourself? These feelings are real even though they may not necessarily be true. Once you reach a certain level of success, these sentiments will still creep in your mind and your heart but you must train yourself to truly believe that you are *More Than Enough*. Success, love, and happiness are in you. It is in you to try something new and to speak up and voice your opinion. Everything you can ever imagine yourself accomplishing is in you.

What is stopping you from living the life you dreamed of? I continuously ask myself, "Jada, what is stopping you from living the life you dream of?" When I sit down, reflect, and dig deep to answer these questions with sincerity, the answer might be doubt, laziness, anxiety, shyness or ignorance. For me, the root of it all is fear. Living, thriving, and being happy is now a necessity to advance to the *next level*. Stepping into a new level of me required me to conquer my fears.

Taking something to the *next level of you* means that you are seeking to further improve or develop something that is already successful. We all have a *next level*. Your *next level* may be deepening spiritual connections, widening your professional reach, or becoming a risk taker. Are you ready to step into the *next level of you*? As you get ready to incorporate fundamental steps from this book, clear your mind and find time in your schedule to devote focused and intentional energy to this journey. You will engage in a process of deep discovery. Some of this discovery may be a little uncomfortable and you may discover bad habits you never knew about yourself. However, there is strength in knowing yourself and power in realizing what needs to shift.

Stepping into the *next level* of you doesn't have to mean more. My *next level* meant chiseling off the excess and focusing on what matters. I assessed my heart, mind, body, and soul to gain a better perspective of what habits, language, and people were necessary to eliminate. On the road to becoming a better me, what mattered was a healthier routine. I craved a more holistic and balanced approach to life. The balancing act was rooted in the examination of toxic habits and an active celebration of growth.

When the idea of writing *More Than Enough* emerged, I thought "How can I help people advance to another level if I am still working to become the best version of me? What do I have to offer?" The book was delayed because of fear, but something about how it felt when I whispered to myself, "You are *More Than Enough*" empowered and affirmed me. My intuition tugged on me to be vulnerable by sharing fears, challenges, and insecurities. I discovered that even though I may not be a finished product people can learn from me while I'm in the process of unearthing. Each one of us has light and life to share that will help grow someone else. The times when I learned the most is when leaders share their truths and areas of growth.

The mantra, *More Than Enough* is powerful and affirming to all.
- You will live a healthier emotional and spiritual life.
- It is all about you and the collective impact.
- You have the tools to change the world.
- You will become a gratitude magnet.
- You break barriers of difference.

How to read this book:

Each chapter begins with fundamental steps for you to utilize throughout your journey to internalize your power. Think about how you can apply these steps to become a better you as you read this text. I'm a firm believer that people learn from their experiences and mistakes. Therefore, I'm thrilled to share stories from my travels in and out of the country. In each experience, there is a lesson. These lessons lead to a guide of how to actualize the fundamental steps of each chapter. At the close of each chapter, you will be challenged to affirm yourself in how you are *More Than Enough*.

Step into the *next level* of you. Do it now. Do not wait. Stay true to you and never forget that you are *More Than Enough*.

*Words with an asterisk are defined in the Glossary.

STEP ONE:
Ask Yourself Why

Reflections in Salvador de Bahia, Brazil

About a week before I traveled to Salvador de Bahia, Salvador, Brazil, a colleague asked me why I chose Brazil to complete my graduate work. The reasons I shared were central to the Africana CHANGE course I was teaching, the study abroad trip I was seeking to develop for students, and the course of research for my graduate school thesis. But there was also a reason that I could not quite put my finger on. It was something more connected to childhood, a distant memory. The country always intrigued me, but I didn't quite know how or when I developed a curiosity for Brazil. I let the unresolved go and figured I would remember sooner or later.

Then it hit me! When I was a teenager, I watched the 1990 movie *The Forbidden Dance* repeatedly. The movie was about Princess Nisa who lived in the Brazilian Amazon. She came to the United States of America to raise awareness about illegal logging and to fight against the huge corporations that were destroying her home. Along her journey she ended up competing in an international dance competition and showing the world her native dance, the Lambada*. Princess Nisa used this as a platform to preserve her culture.

I smiled to myself because I remembered fantasizing about traveling to Brazil to learn more about the Amazon and the Lambada. This was where my "why" was rooted. It hit me at that moment. My "why". The "why" for me coming to Brazil was much more historical than I thought and my "why" connected to my love of learning about culture, education, activism, the arts and connecting those four elements. The plan was to use this learning to inform ways to preserve and celebrate my own culture. I was there to complete graduate research and deliver ways to teach English as a Second Language in a school in a low-income area of Brazil known as a favela. I was also there to incorporate and celebrate Afro-Brazilian culture into the lessons. In the process, I fell in love with Bahia and its rich history.

Bahia Love Affair (2012)
He breathes so much life in everything.
In me he breathes passion.
In me he breathes dreams.
The way he kisses the crevice of my skin.
A smooth forceful motion of waves crashing.
How delightful are his dreamy eyes?
Stars staring into my heart.
My feet dance to the rhythm.
Jinga kinda swag. Samba kinda moves.
Mango sweets & sugar cane spirits.
Sun-kissed skin circle my mind.
His penmanship painting perfect mysteries on canvas.
He has a way of showing up in places I never knew existed.
Jinga kinda swag. Samba kinda moves.

A spirituality that invites spirit, that invites the spirits, that
celebrates love, that celebrates life
He knows how to live like none other.
His smile mirrors the sunset.
A treasure of God.
His laughter can cure cancer.
And his statue cured my broken heart.
Fireworks on taste buds.
I never knew these flavors of the world existed.
I mirror his openness and complexity.
Doors wide open. Curiosity never shuts.
Always becoming.
Always in love with Salvador de Bahia.

• • • • •

    My biggest honor was to make my parents proud. They wanted me to excel academically in school and to strive for excellence. Within the expectation of success, I was also expected to be a respectful, nice, and caring person. Simple, right? But as life continued, specific expectations of parents, family, peers, church members, teachers, and coaches were voiced. Although people around me wanted the best, sometimes other people's ideas about my potential of me blurred my own understanding of my "why." Through various stages of life, it was imperative for me to ask myself on a regular basis, "What is your why?" This pivotal question grounded me and helped me to focus on my reasons for living and my purpose in life. Knowing your why will lead you to creating a path that is the perfect fit for you. You are more than what others have laid out for you to be. You are your wildest dream, but you must discover your why. Begin this process by dismissing the potential, owning your power, and satisfying a need. It is up to you to break through the foundations that have been laid out for you to follow.

Fundamental Steps

- Dismiss the potential
- Own your power
- Satisfy a need

Dismiss The Potential

Concentrate on the YOUR in the phrase "Ask Yourself Why." You do this by dismissing what others think your potential should be and focusing on your own understanding of your potential. Potential is a word that focuses on the possible and likely future. You are the person that needs to develop what your possible future will be like. Sure, you may be great at crunching numbers, or you may be an amazing leader in your community who has shown the skills of organizing or event planning, but this may not be the route that you want to take. Appreciate the compliments given by people around you that are connected to your attributes, but dismiss the comments that people make to you about your potential. You need to clear your mind and think about the potential you have on your own.

People have often told me that I have the potential to be a great political leader. Initially, I thought to myself, "Wow, me a politician?!" I was shocked that others saw this in me because I never really thought about politics as a career path. I began to research the possibilities and the various routes to take to get there, but then I realized that it wasn't a potential route that I wanted to take. Will my mind change in the future? Maybe it will and maybe it won't. I take the compliments and I ask which attributes lend to me being a good politician. Some of the feedback includes my passion for positive change, my abilities as a public speaker, my focus on being an intentional listener and awesome convener of people, and having a strategic mind. I'm appreciative for the skills I've developed. Equally, I think of how to grow those skills for the goals that I want to achieve, not the goals others want me to achieve. People will always share their opinion of who you are and what they feel or think you will accomplish in life, but it is up to you to fulfill your own dreams

What do others place pressure on you to accomplish that you need to dismiss?

_____
_____
_____
_____
_____

What is your reason for getting out of the bed each day?

_____
_____

_____

_____

_____

What is your "why?" What are you passionate about? What is your purpose?

_____

_____

_____

_____

Own Your Power

Each of us is powerful in our own way. The power within is ready to burst at the seams, but for some reason we hold back our power. Some of us hold back because of the fear of moving forward. Some of us hold back due to fear of the unknown. Others hold back because we feel like it is necessary to make others feel good by dimming our light. You are constantly developing amazing gifts given to you by a higher power. It would be shameful to let that go. Talents and gifts drift away when they are not being utilized. Have you ever seen the dilapidation of a perfectly great house that is uninhabited? Just like a vacant house, your power will wither away if you do not own it, sharpen it, and use it with pride.

Remember that those things that make you powerful stem from something, whether it be an event, a person or a class.

For instance, when I really put my mind to it, I'm a great writer. Believe it or not, writing is not my favorite thing to do. As a kid, I was assigned books to read and was expected to write a synopsis of the books each summer. Although I hated it growing up, it's a skill that I possess and can share with others. Great written communication has also come in handy while writing proposals and designing curricula. If I would have completely stopped just because I didn't like writing, I would not have been a successful college student, professional consultant, and author. Because I decided to own my gift for writing, even when I did not like it, I owned my power by making a definitive decision. There will be many things that you *can* do, and you have the power to make decisions about each of them. No matter your decision, it is always important to own your own power.

What are the skills and perspectives that make you powerful? How will you own your power?

_____
_____
_____
_____
_____

Satisfy A Need

Part of the reason we are distracted from our paths is because our "why" is not connected to a strong need. What need are you satisfying in the world with your passion and purpose? We all have a purpose when we are moving throughout life. When action is disconnected from fulfilling a need, the impact is not as meaningful. Advancing to the *next level of you* means that you are cognizant of how your life has meaning for you and for others. Being connected to something greater than you will enhance your energy and zeal for life.

About two years ago, I coached a woman who was extremely successful. She figured out how to cut negativity from her life and realized her own potential. Yet, she always felt a sense of emptiness until she began to fill a need. From conversations with colleagues, she learned that the elders in a nursing home close to her job needed weekly companionship. This companionship was for keeping the residents company as a preventative measure to slow or avert the onset of Alzheimer's disease. As soon as she began to volunteer, her void began to close. Perhaps you believe that there is nothing that you can do on a grand scale to satisfy a need, and because of that belief, you feel that there is no need to try to make a difference at all. Understand that because you are *More Than Enough*, whatever you offer will be beneficial. If you don't have time to regularly visit a nursing home, knit blankets for premature babies, or raise money for a charity, remember that the need you satisfy may be something as simple as a smile to a stranger. Whatever it is, satisfy a need because you will feel more fulfilled.

What need are you filling with your life's work?

_____
_____
_____
_____
_____
_____
_____
_____
_____
_____

Fundamental Steps

- Dismiss the potential
- Own your power
- Satisfy a need

Complete the affirmation and pay it forward by sharing with loved ones and posting on social media with a selfie.

I am #MoreThanEnough because

_____
_____
_____
_____

People will always share their opinion of who you are and what they feel or think you will accomplish in life, but it is up to you to fulfill your own dreams.

STEP TWO:
Reflect Deeply
Reflections in Rich Square, NC

When I was in elementary school, I came home excited about my new teacher Mrs. Francis. I shared this excitement with my parents. Then my dad asked me the weirdest thing, "Did she ever invite you to the pool in her neighborhood?" I was confused and giggled at such a silly question. I said, "No Daddy, we have our own pool. Why would she need to do that and why does that matter? She's nice to me and I like her." He then proceeded to tell me that even though she is nice to me, I have to continue to work twice as hard because I am a woman and because I'm Black. My intelligence and Mrs. Francis' polite nature did not trump the fact that my skin tone is almond colored and her's ivory. This was my first lesson in race, gender, and class.

His message was that Mrs. Francis was nice and that was great, but there was a clear separation between us and societal norms in place to keep our world's detached. Even though my mom and dad were trying to protect me, what I discovered while reflecting on this memory is much more than what is at the surface. The lesson was that people may be well-meaning and nice, but our society has taught others to make life harder for you as a Black woman. This is true in some cases, but there was another lesson that cut even deeper. I am not enough for this world and because I am less than, I should work twice as hard. As difficult as it is, I acknowledge that my parents were a part of the messaging communicating to me that I am not enough. That reality hurts like hell. Yet, on the contrary, they were also key in instilling the message that I am *More Than Enough* by telling me I can accomplish anything I desired.

• • • • •

Allowing time for intense reflection helped me to improve my awareness skills in a way that I never imagined. Thoughtful, strategic and purposeful mindfulness helped me to build the mental toughness required to step into the *next level* of me. Deep reflection requires taking time outs, practicing mindfulness, seeking knowledge, and conquering the inconsistencies. It takes courage to engage in deep reflection because everything you discover about yourself and your story is not always what you want it to be.

Fundamental Steps
- Take a time out
- Practice mindfulness
- Conquer the inconsistencies

Take A Time Out

Imagine constantly behaving as if your time is the most precious thing in your life. To get to where you want to be in life, you must be willing to step away and take a time out. A time out is a mental and/or physical escape from your normal routine to step away to 1: Assess your life, 2: Discover your areas of improvement, 3: Further grow your goals and dreams, and 4: Create a plan for your "why." People may not understand it. Some will even be upset with you for taking time away from them, but without a chance to deeply reflect on yourself, you will be crunched into a never-ending spiral of being busy. The culture of busy breeds the continual dismissal of the need to create space to observe habits and to step into the *next level* of you.

Your time out may be for a day or a 20-year tenure. It all depends on what you need to step into that next level. How bad do you want it? What are you willing to sacrifice to demand a time out?

_____
_____
_____
_____
_____
_____
_____

One of the reasons why I longed to be an entrepreneur was to control my schedule and have more time to spend with loved ones. I was terribly mistaken because entrepreneurship demands more time to develop growth strategy, train employees, recruit and retain clients, and most importantly to deliver excellent service. There were times when I felt extremely sad for missing family gatherings or opportunities to get together with friends. I'm a supporter and nurturer at heart so not being present really bothered me.

Now, I recognize that the route to my "why" is different than other people. My journey isn't as fast as I want it to be, but I'm alright with that. What I am doing for others is enough. I am *more than enough* for those around me. I've learned that when people are cheering for you, they have more empathy for the sacrifices you make to reach your dreams. Truly supportive people don't allow themselves to be time-snatchers; those who drain you of your time and energy without replenishing you. Stay away from them because they will try to make you feel guilty for being driven and focused.

Because I travel so much, when I am in town I tend to take mini time-outs in my home. The love and care emanating through the warm burnt orange, deep lilac, and cream-colored walls help me to relax and recharge. Whether you take a few hours or days or even weeks off work just to get away, do it. Make sure your moments of deep reflection are taken with minimal distractions and include the things that make you happy and keep you focused.

When can you take short and extended time outs in the next 6 months? Schedule time outs in your calendar below.

_____

_____

_____

_____
_____
_____
_____
_____
_____

Practice Mindfulness

 Mental performance mindset coach and sports psychologist Dr. Michael Gervais, says that when you are mindful you are better able to "push on the edges of instability." This is so true in my life because the practice of mindfulness has equipped me to take bigger and more calculated risk during this journey of leveling up. It will be hard for you to push your "edges of instability" if you are not knowledgeable about where those limits are.

 I found myself meditating in the mornings and evenings, yet my mind would continue to race all day. I've found that with the practice of mindfulness, I am more present with how my thoughts align with the way my body feels and I'm better able to control the way my mind thinks and how I react in varying situations. There is more clarity, calmness, and the result is consistency. The reality is simple, without clarity of goals and vision of your future, you will not step into the *next level* of you. Follow these steps to bring about more mindfulness practices.

When there are too many outputs and inputs in a given day, your brain will freeze. Have you ever had a nonstop day full of constant conversations, phone calls, meetings, strategy sessions, etc.? At the end of your day did you feel like you were trapped in a moment of time where you couldn't fathom thinking about anything else or taking anymore phone calls? I remember times when I would have an extremely successful day, yet mentally draining to the point where it took at least 10-30 minutes in pure silence just to get to a place of recollecting my thoughts. It's not like the day wasn't good. Sometimes I'm operating off so much adrenaline that I don't take enough time outs throughout the day to just 'chill', reflect, document, and reboot; in that order. If I have a day of constant commitments, I make it a point to just chill, reflect, document, and reboot before the next thing because after so many inputs and outputs it is very hard to remember what happened during each segment of the day. Here is an example of how to do this throughout your day even if you only have three minutes.

- For 15 seconds, breathe in and out slowly three times. **CHILL**

- Next, for one minute sit in silence and just think about what happened in your day. **REFLECT**

- Then for the next minute, write down a bullet point summary of the take-aways and next steps. **DOCUMENT**

- Lastly, take 45 seconds to move your body around with the intention to generate new energy by stretching, jumping, dancing, opening and closing your eyes, or make silly faces. **REBOOT**

Do not allow notifications to interrupt your mindfulness time! You'll find yourself smiling as you recount the small ray of sunshine that landed on your arm while you were chilly or the smile on the drive thru attendants face as you picked up your order. You will also note the unpleasant things like being ignored at your job during a meeting or the unnerving post you saw on Facebook. You will live in the moment and that is mindfulness; pausing, recounting, and being closer to you. You will leave with better insights of your day or segments of your day that will help you to develop better strategies for tomorrow.

How and when can you practice mindfulness?

_____
_____
_____
_____
_____
_____
_____
_____
_____
_____

Conquer The Inconsistencies

In the example in the reflection, I was aware of how my family wanted to protect me. This teaching is common in Black households. Why is that, you might ask? My father was preparing me for the worst. My family wanted to protect me, and prepare me for a world that was not always in favor of my success. But at the same time, the message was detrimental to my mental health and my overall self-esteem.

I reflected on this message my father and other family members gave me while reading Ta-Nehisi Coates' book, Between the World & Me. Coates says,

> "All my life I'd heard people tell their black boys and black girls to 'be twice as good,' which is to say, 'accept half as much.' These words would be spoken with a veneer of religious nobility, as though they evidenced some unspoken quality, some undetected courage, when in fact all they evidenced was the gun to our head and the hand in our pocket. This is how we lose our softness. This is how they steal our right to smile. No one told those little white children, with their tricycles, to be twice as good. I imagined their parents told them to take twice as much. It seemed to me that our own rules redoubled plunder. It struck me that perhaps the defining feature of being drafted into the black race was the inescapable robbery of time, because the moments we spent readying the mask, or readying ourselves to accept half as much, could not be recovered. The robbery of

time is not measured in lifespans but in moments. It is the last bottle of wine that you have just uncorked but do not have time to drink. It is the kiss that you do not have time to share, before she walks out of your life. It is the raft of second chances for them, and twenty-three-hour days for us."

    In that preparation for the worst, the indirect message was that I wasn't good enough for whoever out there in the world who thought less of me because of my race and my gender. Consequently, my parents told me that I could be and do anything. And you know what? I believed them. Because of my competitive and stubborn nature, I developed the mentality that I am going to show the world out there that I am MORE THAN ENOUGH. Yet, I would hear the noise in the background: You always have to work twice as hard. The double-standard.

    When I read this, it reframed my mind. The thought of losing one hour of each day for my entire life because my parents were simply trying to protect me and prepare me for an unjust world made me mad as hell. I sat and thought about all the moments when I would rethink and recalculate comments. I reflected on the calculated steps I would make in the smallest situations. The continuous overthinking and over strategizing is exhausting to my mind and my body. After reading those words, I vowed to never lose one hour from my day because of feelings of not being enough or having to work twice or three times as hard. If I lost an hour, it would be because I consciously decided to have a lazy day or because I felt like getting extra sleep. I am no longer a slave to subconscious lessons told to me as a child that find ways to creep into my self-worth. I'm reclaiming my time! All 11,315 hours of my life. I may not get it back, but I promise not to lose anymore.

One of the hardest things I've reflected on recently is my career and what it means for me, my why. I'm a diversity and leadership consultant. The formula that I base my LLC on is that Historic Truth Telling + Building Relationships + Creative Action = Social Justice. My background in understanding social justice is deeply rooted in critical race theory*, liberatory consciousness*, and anti-oppressive models. The constant in all the aforementioned philosophies is the notion of perpetual systems of inequity and inequality. These systems include, but are not limited to: judicial (courts, law enforcement), education (k-12, higher education, private, public), health care (urgent care, hospital, clinic, insurance). I whole-heartedly agree with the formula of Social Designs*. Consequently, I've begun to test the historic truth-telling aspect even more.

One of those major areas is testing the stereotypes, notions, and truths about me, a Black woman. One of the hardest things to do is airing 'dirty laundry.' I was taught growing up that family business needs to stay family business. Sometimes I feel caught between holding systems of inequity accountable for many social ills I see within the Black community. Yet, I also see social ills that people in my community create and or perpetuate. Socially, holding ourselves accountable to issues is not ok in the world we live in where we see time and time again videos of young and old people being killed unjustly by people like George Zimmerman or cops who don't even go to trial. I do believe in holding people accountable as well as changing laws and policy that are founded in justice for all. Now that's established, I also believe that communities like Black Wallstreet can happen again. I believe the billions of dollars spent by us in the Black community can actually support Black economies, which will in turn make this country and the world even stronger.

In making my life's work about unpacking systems and helping leaders to change their companies to create more equitable outcomes, I feel like I've been able to merge my passion, my livelihood, and my career. I also feel like I have not done enough to add to the conversation and to take conversations to sometimes unwanted territory. The unwanted territory that I am writing about includes being critical of lower education standards and trends of using 'slay' and 'savage' as words to describe the personality of Black women. In my inconsistency, lies the discomfort. Deep reflection has allowed me to hold many truths at the same time to bring about as much change as I can.

What are tough inconsistencies in your life that you have been afraid or nervous to confront? In what ways have you noticed contradictions in your life, in yourself, and in others? Is it healthy that these inconsistencies live parallel in your life?

_____
_____
_____

_____

_____

_____

_____

_____

After each new phase or life shifting moment, take the needed time to rediscover. Rediscover to develop a new lens of purpose and vision to align yourself with the heightened level you are seeking. When entering a rediscovery phase, more than likely there is something in your previous phase that you will need to let go of. This thing, person, or habit may be good or bad. If positive, you will need to weigh your options. If negative, let it go indefinitely. Sometimes what you are rediscovering may reveal something you were already aware of but with a different perspective. Keep reflecting. When you think you've done enough, you've just scratched the surface.

Fundamental Steps

- Take a time out
- Practice mindfulness
- Conquer the inconsistencies

Complete the affirmation and pay it forward by sharing with loved ones and posting on social media with a selfie.

I am #MoreThanEnough because

_____
_____
_____
_____
_____
_____
_____

It takes courage to engage in deep reflection because everything you discover about yourself is not always what you want to be.

STEP THREE:

Detox

Reflections in Durban, South Africa

We rose at the crack of dawn to travel from our suburban Durban neighborhood to The Valley of 1000 Hills, both in the province of Kwazulu, South Africa. I'd never been engulfed in such an enormous mast of deep green and plush earth. The 90-minute ride to the Intakemazolo Combined School felt like I was journeying closer to God. For as far as you could see, there were hills of never-ending beauty. I wanted to capture this feeling of relief and calm in a bottle and take it back home with me.

We arrived at the school where there were hundreds of smiling children. They were far more mature and present than any private or public school I've visited in the States. The school vision: "a holistically developed child that contributes towards the growth of our community," was deeply inspiring, and it was a pleasure to experience the vision in action with the amazing children studying there. Their smiles were brightest while sharing components of their culture with us. We tapped into our inquisitive nature and were eager to know more about each other. We exchanged words and phrases and taught each other dance moves from traditional

Zulu culture, to the traditional African American Electric Slide, to the Nae-Nae. There was so much beauty in our global connectivity. The tradition of stepping within the historically Black Greek letter organizations in the United States mirrored the traditional warrior movements of the Zulu. The rhythmic tune of our beats matched the down beat of their songs. We also dispelled negative myths about each other through pure interaction and courageous conversations.

Back in the city of Durban, our group of professional women socialized with all types of people; rural farmers, cooks, councilmen, entertainers, drivers, mayors, club owners, teachers, pharmaceutical researchers, magazine editors, photographers, principals, and the list goes on. Each person I met was genuinely interesting in knowing more about my purpose, my joys, my passion. The inquiry of human-to-human interaction was slow, steady, and fulfilling. I wanted to bottle this type of interaction and take this home too. Interactions where there was no ask, there was no expectation; only the hope to learn and to grow. My attention to human interaction and reflection grew while in this amazing country.

After full days and nights of cultural connections, sightseeing, and partying; I was privileged to wake up and watch the sunrise over the Indian Ocean off the southern coast of South Africa. For six days, the Indian Ocean spoke to me with authority and grace. For six days, I listened to the healing sounds of this great body of water. During those quiet moments, my thought processes slowed down. I forced myself to recollect and write down the blessings from that year and to celebrate my accomplishments. The ocean has no end, no beginning, and no boundary and it taught me that no matter what happens life will go on, if I let it. In each obstacle, I can decide to complain about mistakes and wrongdoings, quit or keep living. I decided to bottle every lesson from South Africa and take it home with me.

· · · · ·

It was after election day 2016, and my return to the United States was wrought with the reality of a deeply divided country, and between those beautiful flashbacks of my time in Durban, there were text alerts, emails and so many meetings. This reality quickly pushed my Durban experience out of the existence of my memory. I felt stifled by the idea that there was not much positive change possible in the United States of America. Each day back I was amazed at how much friends, family and colleagues were suffering, afraid, and uninspired. In my line of work, this was the time for me to build curriculum, write response blogs, and be in the midst of political and social action.

I decided that I needed to detoxify my mind. Instead of heeding the call of potential, I heeded the call of detoxification. I retreated. I had to believe that what others had to offer in the form of business and strategy in those moments was *more than enough*. I had to believe that it was worth it to hold onto the piece of happiness I experienced in Durban to continue to grow. For almost 60 days leading into the new year, I decided to take an extended time-out, minimize meetings, maximize family time, and grow.

Fundamental Steps
- Practice purity
- Bounce back from "outages"
- Let go

Practice Purity

Detoxification is the process of removing toxins from your body, but it is also a process aiding in clearing out your mind and increasing your overall health. When toxins or poisons are in your body, you will never reach your highest level of physical health and mental growth. A fit person may look good from the outside, but if their body is full of waste, the toxins just create a barrier for optimal health. In my early twenties if I picked up a few pounds, it was easier to lose the weight than in my late twenties and into my thirties. Even if I tried personal training, two-a-day workouts, or changing my diet, I would not see the same results I noticed earlier in life. Initially, I attributed the challenge to stress, older age, lack of sleep, and relationship issues. I was wrong. The reason for the slow weight loss, moodiness, sleepiness, and overall inability to get to my old self was because over the years my body built up toxins, and I needed to detoxify. I realized this by accident when a friend encouraged me to complete the JJ Smith 10-Day Green Smoothie Cleanse.

As I embarked on the preparation stage of grocery shopping for the list of fresh foods and researching the effects of detoxing, my mind shifted from simply wanting to drop pounds to wanting to start and continue a healthier lifestyle. The detox process taught four major lessons in a short 10-day span; organization, preparation, discipline, and grace.

Organization

The more your systems are in place, the more ordered your steps are each day. Every three days I would plan my grocery, budget, and preparation schedules while completing the detox. It was a must to purchase as much fresh food as possible. It was equally imperative to match my work schedule with my meal schedule to make sure I had the necessary amount of snacks and the proper refrigeration methods for the smoothies if I was 'out and about'. As a result, my calendar, pantry, and even weekly wardrobe was more organized.

Preparation

Plan each day for success so that you will be better prepared for delays or emergencies. Organizing my life more effectively helped me prepare for short and long-term projects. I was amazed how much clearer my mind was based on a few habit changes. I followed up with clients at a quicker pace and I was more equipped to respond to an abrupt schedule change or a client emergency.

Discipline

Stay the course and do not waiver in the methods, habits, and structure in place to accomplish the goals you set for yourself. J.J. Smith cautions people that you will want to give up while completing the cleanse. She says, "Its normal. But I know that sometimes the only way to grow in life is to be uncomfortable. How else do you grow mentally, spiritually, and physically?" I was extremely uncomfortable during the detox period, but after day two I felt great! At day 10, I was stronger, I had more composure in other areas and I was a lot more patient.

Grace

Give yourself permission to make mistakes while striving to reach your goals. Be careful not to solely strive for perfection and leave room for bumps and bruises along the journey. Sometimes being present and intentional is more important than perfection. I would find myself slowing down while detoxing to avoid expending more energy that I was taking into my body. In the process, I had an earlier start in the morning and regulated my bedtime more frequently. About five of the 10 days, I went to the gym to workout. Afterward on day seven, I was lightheaded and needed more substantial food. I decided to eat a small portion of chicken. Instead of feeling like I didn't make it to the end without meat, I celebrated the fact that I made it all the way to day seven without quitting.

What do you need to organize in your life? How will organizing this area have a ripple effect in other areas in your life?

_____

_____

_____

Choose a day of the week to plan two things; 1- your upcoming week and 2- steps to reach a specific long- term goal?

_____
_____
_____
_____
_____

How can you be more disciplined? Name a time when you were not disciplined. What can you do now to avoid wavering in the future?

_____
_____
_____
_____
_____

How can you allow for more grace and invite more opportunities for being intentional and present?

_____
_____
_____
_____
_____

Bounce Back From "Outages"

I have what I call "re-occurring back outages." On any given day and at any given moment, I'll feel a sharp pain or a dull crippling pain in my back. No matter how much I work out, strength train, do Yoga or Pilates, or visit the chiropractor, the outages happen. What's most annoying is that I'll be in a groove. I'm talking a 3-9-month groove and all of a sudden it happens. Sometimes it's so bad that I can't even get out of bed, but at other times I can suck it up and withstand the pain. When I sit down in a low chair or sofa on an occasion when I'm having an outage, it hurts to even breathe when I attempt to get up because the pain is so deep and annoying. It is like no matter how bad I try to avoid it, an outage strikes again. It seems like it always happens when I'm close to a fitness goal, important training or a huge deadline.

Different obstacles may come your way that you are not expecting. Roll up your sleeves and get ready to do the hard work by pushing through even when you are out of your comfort zone. The best way to bounce back from setbacks is to prepare yourself for the worst. This year I decided that I am more than the pain. I am more than my obstacle and I will conquer my body. One of the first steps was detoxing which led to a 9-pound weight loss and less pressure on my back. I then decided to enroll in a high intensity and heavy weightlifting fit class. At first, I hesitated because of my history of outages. I didn't want to feel less than anyone else in class if I needed modifications based on my injuries. I felt like I was too weak and not agile enough because of previous surgeries on both knees. Nonetheless, a few people encouraged me and it's been paying off! I've been sore, but no back outages to date. I've also trained myself mentally to ignore the pain and concentrate on the goal ahead, a healthy and fit body.

What can you do to prepare yourself from predicted outages?

_____

_____

_____

_____

What are potential outages that may come your way?

_____

_____

_____

_____

Let Go

If you have a lot of clutter in your space, your life, and in your mind, you will stunt your productivity. When I realized this, my 'clutter-bug' habits went out the window. I cleared everything in my office and house that did not inspire me. I like to keep everything. I keep old pictures, old journals, old clothes, and expired contacts in my phone. But you know what? Letting go to get to the next step is necessary. When you let go of 'baggage,' you allow room for bigger and better dreams. The day I let go of people, things, and even clothes that no longer inspired me was the day my purpose was clearer and my vision sharper.

The practice of letting go creates more mental space for you to think and in the process, relieves stress. After dropping negative eating habits through the 10-Day detox and building the physical capacity of my body, the added level of letting go was a bonus. I had more energy, I could feel my waistline peeking through, and my skin became more vibrant. I'm *still* glowing. I went through my cell phone, email and associate and friend lists to figure out who I needed to step away from. That was extremely hard to do. When you are living day-to-day, it's hard to understand who and what is good for you. If you have those habits that are created, they may blind you to what you need and what makes you healthy. I encourage you to detox, not only for your body but also for your mind and your spirit.

Detoxing from people means that you are getting rid of those who do not nourish you. Some may think that is selfish, but I think the strategy is common sense. We don't eat food that does not replenish us. Why would you want friends who don't do the same? When you detoxify your mind, body, and spirit it becomes clear that you are *More Than Enough*. You see I didn't like being home because my relationship was in shambles and being held together by ragged wire. I was subconsciously yearning to get away to avoid any feelings or the reality that things needed to end with someone who was still a great friend. I went way past my expiration date because there was not enough deep reflection time built into my daily schedule like I mentioned in the previous chapter.

Moreover, I was in a daze and on autopilot because I had not taken the opportunity to detox regularly. When you find the sources of doubt in your life, you are more equipped to survive haters and those internal places that are not serving you well. When we consume food that does not replenish us, what does that do? It may give us a feeling of being full, but in reality, we are full of junk!

Name 5 things and 5 people that you need to let go IMMEDIATELY.

_____
_____
_____
_____

Fundamental Steps
- Practice purity
- Bounce back from "outages"
- Let go

Complete the affirmation and pay it forward by sharing with loved ones and posting on social media with a selfie.

I am #MoreThanEnough because

_____
_____
_____

If you have a lot of clutter in your space, your life, and in your mind; you will stunt your productivity.

STEP FOUR:
Start a Journey of Research
Reflections in Hi Camp, California

We traveled to Hi Camp, a cozy cabin nestled in the mountains of northern California. Lizette, Tarah, and I were in en route to meet the other half of our crew; Wade, Maketa, Benjie, and Teddy, who were traveling down from Seattle, Washington. Gazing out of the window admiring the deep green northern California landscape, I smiled at myself for being adamant and consistent in my quest to be a part of the Youth Action Project (YAP) facilitation team. About six months prior to the road-trip to Hi Camp, I witnessed a powerful presentation by youth from around the nation who shared the impact of YAP in their lives and how the experience prepared them to lead social justice initiatives in their communities. Immediately, knowing that I wanted to be a part of the YAP team, I emailed my resume to Lizette and Tarah because I wanted to become a volunteer facilitator. Because of my persistence and prior experience as a diversity facilitator, I was welcomed to the team as the youngest and only North Carolinian. I stepped outside of my comfort zone to experience a new and challenging endeavor.

Our journey began in San Francisco and we traveled for

three hours telling stories and getting to know each other. The experiences they shared blew me away. I was privileged to begin a journey of learning with two powerful and seasoned social justice educators and couldn't wait to meet the rest of the team. When we made it to Hi Camp, we settled into the two-story cabin surrounded by beautiful trees, animals, and the sound of a distant creek which led to a waterfall. The goals of our retreat were to bond, evaluate the current youth leadership program, and design a new curriculum model for YAP. As the newest and youngest of the crew, I knew that this was a training ground for me to step into the *next level* of me.

We created a balanced environment and a healthy retreat 'vibe' that was conducive to guaranteeing reflection, productivity, and community building. Whenever the opportunity presented itself, I would ask questions of the team to get to know them. I was inquisitive and wanted to soak up as much knowledge as possible. Throughout our intense planning moments, the seasoned professionals encouraged me to share my perspectives and innovation for the curriculum design. I appreciated the extra push because it encouraged me to step into that *next level* of design and development. We bonded while cooking and sharing family recipes. The traditional North Carolinian fried corn bread was the retreat favorite and to this day the team reminisces about it. In between strategy sessions we took individual reflection breaks and hiked together.

Before our last day together, we hiked along a beautiful stream and up the mountain. It was a bit chilly, but we were determined to see the view. The beauty of Hi Camp still amazes me. There were huge light grey stones etched in the hills. Birds from different species chirped and flew from tree to tree. The leaves were beginning to turn on some of the trees and others were evergreens. I was nervous about losing my balance as the altitude increased because of previous knee surgeries and almost turned back, but I kept going. It was worth it too! The reward was the view, cute pictures, and most of all the opportunity to bond with some of greatest teachers I've ever met. I'll never regret taking a leap of faith that led to 1: a journey of research that deepened my passion for educating, and 2: the creation of one of the most powerful frameworks for youth leadership in social justice.

· · · · ·

Being *More Than Enough* is more than just a statement. You must be dedicated to constantly dedicating time to become your best self. Discovering who you are requires research. As much as I think I know who I am, I'm frequently discovering something new. Even though I can be 'hard-headed' and stubborn, I'm on a journey to train myself to be in a constant state of inquiry. Fundamental steps in crafting your journey of research include developing an inquisitive mindset, planting seeds, and asking for help.

Fundamental Steps

- Develop an inquisitive mindset
- Plant the seeds
- Don't be afraid to ask for help

Develop An Inquisitive Mindset

You don't know what you don't know. We all have that in common. Similarly, we don't know everything. Advancing to the *next level of you*, includes having a hunger for knowledge and being addicted to learning. No matter the venue there is always an opportunity to learn. One of the biggest mistakes that I've made was thinking that there was little to nothing to learn when I was in unfamiliar or uncomfortable environments. If I felt like the presentation style was boring or if the person delivering the message offered knowledge in a less than dynamic manner, I would direct only 10-20% of my listening ear and attention. I did not have an inquisitive mindset. I would basically ignore portions of the presentation and indirectly disrespect the presenter. Ultimately, I was denying myself the opportunity for growth. Every teacher or presenter will not cater to your learning style. Therefore, developing the skills to adjust your listening ear and your attention is imperative. Shift your mindset and stay inquisitive even when it is difficult.

How do you do this? An increased level of self-reflection requires you to be a 'hungry' seeker of knowledge. Deep reflection taught me to prepare myself before entering learning environments that I know are not as interactive as I would like them to be and to soak up as much knowledge as possible. I would go into meetings or seminars with my preparation kit; snacks, colorful pens for doodling, and all cell phone notifications turned off. It took a while to train my brain and my patience, but it was worth it. Now, I can be fully present and the information sticks! Furthermore, the high level of attentiveness and focus draws others into you. Because of this, people ask more direct questions or spark up conversations during breaks. Expanding my mind and putting specific practices in place to seek and respect knowledge in a different way is literally changing the way my brain absorbs information and the way I connect with people.

How can you sharpen your attentiveness and become a 'hungry' seeker of knowledge?

_____

_____

_____

_____

_____

_____

_____

_____

_____

Making the decision to resign from my '9 to 5' was scary and required an inquisitive mindset. I needed to research the process for stepping into the *next level*. I was in the higher education industry for 8 years and knew that I wanted to grow Social Designs, my independent consulting business. Courageously, I took the leap of faith, but not before I researched the process of advancing my then eight-year-old business. Even though I was a seasoned business owner, I did not have the experience of running the consultant firm full-time. My goal was to create innovative growth strategies while researching best practices for leadership and diversity professional development. Fear was present but I had to push past my fears by constantly saying to myself, "I am *More Than Enough*." The action after the mantra involved an investigative exploration of my field. I predicted certain business and training scenarios, researched best practices in facilitation, and learned about varying levels of diversity. Developing an inquisitive mindset calmed my fears and produced a successful business model. I encourage you to go forth with an inquisitive mindset by engaging in seeking knowledge. You can start by watching instructional videos, listening to podcasts, reading books, and sparking conversations with people.

Building an inquisitive mindset takes practice. What topics do you need to investigate that will help you step into the *next level of you*? **Write down how often you will seek more knowledge in the next 30 days.**

_____
_____
_____
_____
_____
_____

Plant The Seeds

When planting seeds becomes a part of who you are, you will reap anticipated and unanticipated returns that align with your why. Stepping into the *next level of you* requires you to invest in your future. If you calculated the amount of seeds you invested in your goals, what would be the outcome? Are you planting the seeds for success? The key to planting seeds is being intentional about aligning your investments with your short and long-term goals.

In 2007 when Social Designs launched, I decided to invest 10% of my income and up to 20 hours of time per month to grow the company and to grow my skill level, while working full-time. There was much to learn and much to give. In the next 20 years, my goal was to have one of the top leadership and diversity firms in the world. To make this dream a reality, I needed to invest and give back.

Most of the investment went towards research and professional development. I signed up for business seminars and certification classes that taught me the foundations of developing and growing a business. I learned so much while attending conferences about diversity and leadership. Each month I would reach out to past colleagues or close friends who expressed their professional development challenges to me and offer leadership and diversity trainings for free as a part of the 20 hours per month. Even though the trainings were pro bono, I gained experience and insight about several industries. Over the years, we have continued to work with some of the same companies and they continue to refer Social Designs to their colleagues.

As you build, devote resources and time to your dreams and into other people, the harvest will return. The concept of 'reaping what you sow' is rooted in many cultures and religions. Just as you benefit positively from planting seeds of time and resources, you will benefit negatively if you plant seeds of negativity.

What seeds do you need to plant today to reap positive outcomes and accomplished goals?

_____

_____

_____

_____

_____

_____

_____

_____

Don't Be Afraid To Ask For Help

Even though we teach children to be inquisitive and to ask questions, we do not value that in adults. We expect each other to always be in the know. How will we ever learn if we are always in the know? For example, in the diversity field, you are expected to know the up-to-date politically correct terms and the reasons for any changes. In the leadership field, you are expected to know about all leadership assessment tools. I think it is ridiculous how we chastise people for not knowing. Don't get me wrong, I know that there are basic nuggets of knowledge necessary to perform in a specific industry. However, we must give grace when others are in their arc of learning.

Ask for help when you need it. As you are discovering or re-discovering yourself, understand the journey needs to include others. Believe in yourself enough to have the courage to ask people for help. Asking for help means that you are humble enough to admit when you do not have the information. If you are not wired this way, practice before you approach people and make sure that when you are asking for help that you are ready to listen to the answers. I am guilty of asking people for assistance with an idea or information about a particular industry, but already having the answer in my mind. This prevented me from gaining wisdom and guidance from others. I was a know-it-all, but knew much of nothing. Don't make that mistake. Fish do not know they are fish in water because they are swimming in it. Things were brought to my attention and I either ignored or denied perspectives based on my own understanding. Make sure that you clear your mind and are ready to soak up every ounce of new knowledge.

During this process, I met tons of people that helped me understand the cultural practices and fiscal seasons of their industries. I met people who made decisions within their companies about who to hire for their professional development needs. They shared the criteria necessary for contractors and the process for applying for projects and replying to requests for proposals. A simple internet search or reading through pamphlets did not offer this wealth of knowledge. I had to ask others in order to learn the best ways to offer my specific services of leadership and diversity training. After about a year of research, I created a six-month plan to put this new information into a business growth strategy.

What research do you need to gather? Who do you need to contact? When will you contact them?

_____
_____
_____
_____
_____
_____
_____

Fundamental Steps
- Develop an inquisitive mindset
- Plant the seeds
- Don't be afraid to ask for help

Complete the affirmation and pay it forward by sharing loved ones and posting on social media with a selfie.

I am #MoreThanEnough because

_____
_____
_____
_____
_____
_____
_____

An increased level of reflection requires you to be a 'hungry' seeker of knowledge.

STEP FIVE:

Trust the Expiration Date

Reflections in Jada's Juke Joint, Greensboro, NC

Before heading out to the airport I made sure to dress cute and casual, because you never know who you might run into. I may meet a client in a casual conversation and first impressions are everything. Plus, I feel good when I look good and who knows, I can run into an ex or future husband.

I boarded the tiny Airbus plane out of Terminal B at the Reagan National Airport. The plane was so tiny that I had to duck a little when I stepped inside. At this point, I was over being in tight quarters and away from home. Hoping to have a row to myself, to stretch my 5'9" body, I scooted over to the window seat and peeked out over the wing, daydreaming about being back home, in "Jada's Juke Joint."

Jada's Juke Joint is my home and where solace and happiness lives. The décor breathes Southern posh with touches of warmth and sprinkles of sassiness. After a rough breakup, I redecorated and renamed the house to symbolize the birth of a healthier and more courageous me.

Although traveling broadens my perspective and my

world view, home is grounding and makes me feel whole again. Staring over, under, and through the clouds escalating thousands of miles in the sky, I yearned to listen to Michael Jackson's *Off the Wall* and Smoky Robinson's *Where's the Smoke* records on the record player. I craved the smell of candles and incense burning while preparing a southern home-cooked meal. In 14 days, I had traveled from Greensboro to New York City, to DC and back to Greensboro. I was exhausted and I could not wait to love on Jada's Juke Joint.

When I arrived home, I dropped my bags in the foyer, washed my hands, and started on the meal I had been dreaming up on the plane ride. I decided to cook pan crusted shrimp, sautéed spinach, seasoned brown rice, roasted sweet potatoes, and banana pudding. When I reached for the cornmeal, I realized it expired. "Ugh! Dang it! I really wanted that good ol' House Autry flavor on my shrimp," I shouted to myself. Last year I discovered how amazing lightly sprinkled cornmeal tastes on shrimp after sautéing it for a couple of minutes. I was thinking about this flavor and texture the entire plane ride. I decided to 'keep it pushing' and sautéed the shrimp, while singing along with Michael and Smoky. I was immersed in the grove of the juke joint!

As each part of the meal was cooking and the aroma filled the house, I looked through the rest of the pantry for other expired items. Gosh, was I shocked! Canned beans, flour, almonds, and even grits were expired. I probably threw away two grocery bags of food and absolutely hated throwing the things away. Even more so, I hated being wasteful. I wondered how often I would see those items in the pantry and subconsciously knew it was time to use it or toss it. How often did I let the items pile up because I was in a rush or didn't feel like cooking?

My dinner was almost finished and I couldn't wait to eat after such a long day. While waiting for the last few minutes, I continued looking at a few of the expired items I put to the side. I thought, "Maybe some of the items could still be used and I should test the expiration date." Although I did shake and smell some of the items, I realized that I needed to stop wasting time and trust the expiration date. When it is time to let go, it is time to let go.

• • • • •

I don't like throwing things away, and definitely don't enjoy ending relationships, but holding onto things and people that clearly have expiration dates in your life is detrimental. I want everything to stay the same. But just as seasons change, people, places, and life changes too. Knowing this does not make the growing pains stop. However, prolonging the process of letting go and holding on to what has expired can make a person mentally, emotionally, and physically sick. The same way expired food is poisonous, expired things and people in your life are harmful to your future.

There are two take-aways I learned that night in the pantry; 1- Don't overlook blessings because they may go stale and become useless to you, and 2- let go of unnecessary baggage that may hinder you from your blessings. When God blessed me with certain talents, like athletic ability, I did not train as much as I should have and suffered from injuries. When I didn't let go of the 'baggage' of an unproductive and poisonous relationship, parts of my soul became stagnant.

The gifts and talents you possess are enough for your survival, but when you fail to honor those gifts by failing to grow, you miss out on becoming the best you. Strive to be *more than enough*, because you are. Build a habit of putting an expiration date on everything, pay attention to signs, and sharpen your 'BS' meter.

Fundamental Steps

- Put a date on everything
- Don't ignore the signs
- Sharpen your BS meter

Put A Date On Everything

Live the life you know you are destined to live by examining everything around you. After the examination, put an expiration date on your goals, relationships, and career trajectory. There was a time when the center of my life was supporting and advocating for youth and families who were experiencing homelessness. My hours were spent training volunteers, researching curriculum methods for after-school programs, and connecting people to resources. It was a joy for me to build relationships and community with so many people. I learned from the families and about systems of poverty. I had gratitude for being appreciated by the organization we worked with, volunteers I lead, and the families with whom we worked. Moreover, I loved knowing that we were a part of creating sustainable solutions for people in my community.

Toward the fourth year of working with many amazing people, I knew that the work needed an expiration date. Not because poverty magically ended, but because I knew my skill set evolved to work on policy dedicated to the long-term elimination of poverty. When I made the decision to set the expiration date it was awfully hard. I invested so much in the work and relationships, but I learned in the process that the work I put in and relationships I made were not null and void when my time expired. I simply transferred skills into the *next level* of my work. In each career path, put a date on it from the very beginning. How long will you stay? How will you enhance others and other communities? What do you seek to learn and how will you grow? These are questions that I now ask myself when I begin a new project or a job.

What do you need to learn more about to continue your growth?

_____

_____

_____

_____

_____

Think of a moment when you knew it was time to end a relationship or project and you ignored your own wisdom to do it. Much of what stops us from concluding things in our lives is our fear of the unknown, failure, disappointing others, or even success. Whatever you are afraid of, be bold and tackle your fears head-on. How can you do this?

Write down the challenges of going beyond your expiration date.

_____
_____
_____
_____
_____
_____
_____
_____

Ask yourself, "What pain, hurt, and exhaustion will occur if I do not find resolve?

_____
_____
_____
_____
_____
_____
_____
_____

If I "fail," what would I have learned in the process?

_____
_____
_____
_____
_____
_____
_____
_____
_____

Don't Ignore The Signs

You know the feeling you get when it is time to leave a party or event? It's like a tug to go, though you are not exactly sure why you are feeling it. Viscerally, you may feel anxious or unsettled. For some reason, you ignore the feeling and then something happens like a snagging a nail or getting in an unnecessary argument with a friend. Well in my case, I totaled my car.

Let me tell you what happened. Before heading out of town for a work trip, I was to attend my great-nephew's 1st birthday party, get together for a quick hello with friends in the city, then get on the road by 6pm to make my flight. The birthday party was too cute! My niece and her husband did a marvelous job hosting and the baby enjoyed his celebration with friends, neighbors, and family. I was on 'cloud nine' because almost all my nieces and nephews were together. My one year old great-nephews, Logan and Julian, were checking each other out while playing with their respective toys. The birthday boy was on a major sugar high falling and wobbling all over the place, but determined to stay awake. The new moms, Whitney and Paris, were taking in the joy of seeing their boys together. I caught up with my other nieces. Being around them brings me so much joy.

The party ended and 25 minutes later I was with friends sipping tea and catching up in the heart of downtown Charlotte, North Carolina, right in the midst of the Taste of Charlotte. When we departed ways around 5ish, instead of getting my 'happy behind' on the highway, I decided to enjoy the festivities downtown just for 20 minutes because I had a little time to kill. As I was making this decision, I had a feeling it wasn't the best idea because I still needed to pack and review training notes for my work trip the next day. Still, I ignored that feeling and enjoyed the festival with my friend and her family.

About 30 minutes later, I realized that it was time for me to head back home. Now, not only did I not listen to my intuition, but I was now leaving during a time when traffic would be at its peak. I said to myself, "Something told me to go ahead and leave." Then, BOOM! I got in a car accident. Thank goodness it was not serious as far as injuries, but my car was totaled. I should have listened to the signs to leave when I felt it in my spirit. When you get the feeling, please take heed and listen to it.

What signs are you ignoring in your life?

_____
_____
_____
_____
_____
_____
_____
_____
_____

What changes do you need to make to avoid a potential accident or bad decision in life?

_____
_____
_____
_____
_____
_____
_____
_____
_____

Sharpen Your BS Meter

The same way you are building the capacity to listen to yourself more, listen to the direct and indirect messages people give you too. An unknown author of the following quote presented a light-bulb moment for me, "Never get mad at someone for being who've they have always been. Be upset for not coming to terms with it sooner." When I've ignored the signs of another person's 'BS' in the past, the result was either wasted time or hurt feelings.

What is a BS meter? It's the capability to measure how often someone blatantly lies, tells a fragrant untruth, or an obvious fallacy. A BS meter comes into action when you know that things are just not right around you. It could be a person, it could be a vibe, or a certain situation. Your BS Meter can be a source of protection. The deeper the reflection in practice, the more I am in tune with my surroundings and other people. In past intimate relationships, I allowed things to go over my head; like 'sugarcoated' lies or miscommunication trends. Because I was too busy, I allowed a lot of things to get past my BS meter and to become oblivious to the obvious. Other factors threatened a sharp BS meter and I had to ask myself very hard questions.

Am I worth more than this? Is better possible?

I learned to measure my facts against feelings. In the past, I've continued to deal with people in my life long past their expiration dates, including friends and partners. I kept dealing with BS because a part of me loved the people in my circle and a part of me didn't feel that I could do better. But I accepted that I did not need to entertain anyone's BS to be happy. In fact, I am *More Than Enough,* and for that reason alone, I must always protect what I allow into my heart, mind and spirit. Sharpen your BS Meter and do not settle for anyone that does not feed positively into your life. People who threaten your happiness should no longer be invited to your life. If you do not feel comfortable stepping away completely, watch them even more and prepare yourself for a life without them because in the long run they may not be for you and were only meant to be in your life for a season.

Think about a time when you wish you would have sharpened your BS meter. What could you have done differently? What can you do in the future to sharpen your BS meter?

_____

_____

_____

_____

_____

What is it about me hindering me from noticing BS in myself?

Sharpening your BS meter also means unlearning character traits of your own. My daddy used the phrase, "They got some sh*t with them." He always told me that I had some with me too. I didn't know what it meant as a pre-teen and teenager, but I get it now. I've always been extremely persuasive and he would notice how I would charm and persuade him and my mom to get new clothes or to hang out with friends. The trait of being persuasive can easily transform into manipulating others. A close friend pointed this out to me last year and it was a huge growth moment. I became more cautious of making sure my intentions and actions were communicated as transparent as possible in relationships.

Selfishness is a character flaw that is imperative for me to unlearn. Selfishness is defined as seeking or concentrating on one's own advantage, pleasure, or well-being without regard for others. To be fair and to give myself grace, I am a giving person. However, what I'm learning is that even though I am giving, I am at the center of most of my thoughts, actions, and words. Initially, when this was brought to my attention, I was very defensive and thought to myself, "How dare they tell me I'm selfish? I'm a very giving person." Now I am working to unpack the root of what's hindering me from noticing the BS in me. A couple of things that I've realized is that I grew up very privileged, was the only child in my home, and the youngest of most of my cousins.

Being privileged limited my ability to consistently see and *feel* life circumstances different from my own. I will never know what the phrase, 'humble beginnings' means in its true sense because I have always lived a very comfortable life. With that, there is an expectation for me to have any and everything I want and if I don't get it I'll wonder, "What's wrong with people? Don't they know I am supposed to get what I want?" These realizations are hard to come to terms with, but very important for me to address because I want my intentions to match my impact on others.

Have you ever heard a phrase or a song in a specific moment of your life and it meant so much based on what you were learning about yourself? This happened to me. The song Duckworth by Kendrick Lamar begins with the phrase, "It was always me versus the world, until I found it's me versus me." Reflect Deeply about your areas of BS internally that may be creating a you versus the world complex. You may be your worst detour away from success, not someone else.

Name a character trait that you need to improve or unlearn. What are the steps you will take to be a better you?

_____

_____

_____

_____

Fundamental Steps
- Put a date on everything
- Don't ignore the signs
- Sharpen your BS meter

Complete the affirmation and pay it forward by sharing with loved ones and posting on social media with a selfie.

I am #MoreThanEnough because

_____

_____

_____

_____

If you have a lot of clutter in your space, your life, and in your mind; you will stunt your productivity.

STEP SIX:

Unplug

Reflections in El Roblè, El Salvador

The El Roblè village of El Salvador, Central America removed me from of my comfort zone. There was no cell phone service, no Wi-Fi, no television, and no computer. I was in a tucked away community and unplugged from the rest of the world. Here, it was easier to stay focused on the "here and now" of growing, learning, and connecting. I was inspired to listen to the rhythm of my heart beat and focus on the movement of my mind. Being in El Roble gave me peace. Each morning the roosters would do their earthly duty and wake everyone. At first, I hated it, but missed the natural alarm clock by the time I returned home. Walking almost a mile to rebuild the village school that was destroyed during the civil war brought a sober joy. At 7:30am, the temperature was nice and cool before the afternoon heat index kicked in and it was mornings when I could see and smell the fresh dew painting a new beginning to each day. It was a breath of fresh air to unplug from my normal routine.

Most people would wave and say, "Buenos Días," with a huge smile. Others would give an acknowledging glare, maybe wondering who this stranger was in their neighborhood.

During our breaks from rebuilding, elders told stories and taught us Spanish. In the afternoons, we enjoyed sitting on the grass in front of the field, watching the youth and adults play soccer when they returned from school and work, respectively. It was refreshing to smile, laugh, and cheer for everyone. The residents invited our study abroad group to play and one day I obliged. That wasn't a pretty sight to see because my soccer skills absolutely sucked. Nonetheless, it was fun and everyone was so encouraging.

The walk back to my temporary home was just as enriching as the national pastime. People would stop me on the way to converse about the day, politics, global economics, ethnic histories, and relationships. Normally, my mind is always busy, but in El Salvador it began to slow down. Unplugging from technology and routine obligations offered a breath of fresh air that I truly needed to become more in sync with myself, nature, and the community.

There, it was customary to talk to each other, ask questions, and simply 'vibe' in the yard until the sun went down. I loved it. The sound of the swaying trees soothed me and the noises of the animals nearby created a natural playlist. Sometimes before heading out to dinner and reflection, my host family and I would chat about each other's culture in 'Spanglish.' My host Dad spoke a good amount of English and I spoke a little Spanish. While swaying in the hammock, I'd thumb through the Spanish-to-English dictionary to translate unknown words. I'm grateful for the opportunity to unplug from my life long enough to build intercontinental and intercultural connections and to plug into an experience that forced me out of my comfort zone.

• • • • •

Fundamental Steps
- Be in sync
- Mind your business
- Explore nature

Be In Sync

Be in sync with yourself and the universe. Work to be in sync with God, not social media, trends, hot topics, but with God. I've found an inner peace with what is and what will be. We sometimes get so wrapped up in keeping up and performing that we do not take care of self. I asked myself one day, what would the world be like if there were no cell phones, planes, music, or television? What would the world be like without constant contact with the world around you?

Imagine leaving all your technology devices home while running errands or while at work. How much free time would you have to be in sync with your thoughts and your feelings? For seven days, a friend and I tried to leave our devices home while out of the house. It was difficult at first because we built a habit of listening out for notifications, checking email, or group texting throughout the day. A few days I cheated because I wanted to track miles and listen to music while jogging. Those days I jogged without my phone, I noticed a difference. The experience was whole as my thoughts and the sounds of nature were clearer. There weren't as many interruptions and I felt a sense of calmness. After our seven-day experiment, I wanted to know why it was so hard to break the habit of being so attached to my cell phone. In my research, I found a book that changed my perspective of myself and helped me to unplug more often.

In *The Power of Habit*, Charles Duhigg explains the influence of habits in our lives, the process of how they develop, and he shares tools for starting and stopping habits. One of the major scientific discoveries is the basal ganglia, a part of the brain that is "central to recalling patterns and acting on them. It stores habits even while the rest of the brain goes to sleep." Moreover, habits operate in a three-step pattern called the Habit Loop. "First there is a cue, a trigger that tells your brain to go into automatic mode… then there is the routine, which can be physical or mental or emotions… finally there is a reward, which helps your brain figure out if this particular loop is worth remembering."

When I read this, it made so much sense to me. I needed to 'Reflect Deeply' to figure out what the reward was in my habit loop and to discover new rewards as I sought new and healthier habits. I wanted to be in sync with myself, instead of allowing unhealthy habits to run my life. For an additional 30 days, I experimented with different actions and rewards. Two things that came out of this journey of research was 1: I did not look at my phone in the morning first thing anymore and 2: I wrote in a journal to recount my thoughts from the day before for at least 20 minutes. The rewards were an increased level of mindfulness and a more informed analysis about myself.

Name a couple unhealthy habits you need to break. What are the Habit Loops of those habits? What are steps you can take for the next 30 days to be more in sync with yourself?

_____
_____
_____
_____
_____
_____
_____
_____
_____
_____
_____

Mind Your Business

The phrase "mind your business" typically means to respect someone else's privacy. At the root of this phrase, there is a request for individuals to take control of and be in sync with their own lives. Minding your business takes two parts:

Unpack Your Insecurities

If not careful, it is possible to bury opportunities to develop long-term partnerships and relationships by not minding or 'tending to' your own insecurities. Remember that you are more than your insecurities. Who you are and what you offer of yourself is amazing. What you offer the world is unique and it cannot be duplicated. Unplug long enough to be by yourself to unpack those insecurities and habits that are stunting your success.

When I was in college I felt intimidated by a young woman, though I didn't know I was intimidated at the time. This woman had her 'ducks in a row.' She dressed fashionably and attended an HBCU (Historically Black College/University), which in my mind meant that she was 'conscious'. She was a great leader and a powerful speaker. I admired her so much and wanted to be close to her and get to know her. As we grew older, our paths went different ways. One path was not greater or better than the other, each path just transpired differently. She moved to another country to fulfill dreams. I stayed in the US and began to travel often. Both of our paths included motivating others, diversity, leadership, and entrepreneurship.

Instead of being intimidated, I should have been in the business of unpacking my own insecurities, which were entrenched in a few things. I was self-conscious about my weight, which in turn made me self-conscious about my clothes and fashion choices. I also wondered what life would be like if I attended an HBCU and sometimes envisioned a more grounded understanding of my African-American history. After connecting with this same woman years later, I realized that my insecurities got in the way developing a strong relationship. We were associates during our undergraduate years and were often associated with similar circles, but never deepened the connection. I subconsciously kept our relationship at a distance to protect my insecurities. I was afraid to get close to this woman, partly because I was not fully secure in who I was and where I wanted to go in life. Years later, our connection is so rich and inspiring. I realized my insecurities, 'checked myself,' and now I know that I am *more than enough.*

What is it about you and your insecurities that is keeping you from taking care of business? What steps will you take to overcome your insecurities?

_____
_____
_____
_____
_____
_____
_____
_____

_____

_____

Limit Your Attention to Others' Lives

The second tier of minding your business is not worrying about what others are doing with their lives. The way social media is designed and perpetuated by users is for us to feel extremely connected to others based on what we see on our digital screens. The purpose is to stay connected, I get it; however, spending hours 'lurking', spying, and trying to figure out what is really going on in the lives of others is a waste of time. Did you know that recent studies show that the average person will potentially waste up to five years or more in their lifetime on social media? Think about how much you can accomplish in five years or what new skills you can develop. You cannot step into the *next level* of you by paying too much attention to other people.

What new skill, craft, or knowledge can you gain by limiting your social media usage?

_____

_____

_____

_____

_____

_____

_____

_____

_____

Explore Nature

The joyous feeling I experienced in El Roblè, El Salvador comes back to me when I just stop to take in my surroundings. I've made a habit of engaging in physical activity at least once per week outside. I may jog, stretch, play basketball, or play on a playground. Regardless of the activity, when I finish, I feel like all my senses are heightened. My vision is clearer, I can hear better, and my sense of awareness is sharper.

My creativity is fueled by the serenity of nature. During each business trip, it is mandatory for me to explore the unique parts of nature in every city visit. I recall one visit when I traveled to Denver, Colorado. Near our hotel there was a beautiful trail that led to a massive view of the snow-covered mountains. It was like looking at miles and miles of sky high softness. I remember taking in the view and experiencing such a profound connection to nature. My mind started racing and I distinctly recall brainstorming an entire virtual summer camp curriculum in leadership and diversity for teachers. The ideas came rushing faster than the nearby jogger. Unplugging and going closer to nature calmed me and I was more present with my thoughts.

Research a few natural parks and sites in your city or state for you to explore in the next six months.

Unplugging is necessary for growth. Find time to unplug and to focus on you. When you unplug, you protect your energy. Sometimes, something or someone will take your energy to an entirely different place than what you intended. You want to have a level-head and a calmness about you when you decide to complete important tasks, projects, or planning. When I made unplugging a life practice, I developed better breathing techniques and my connection to God deepened. The more I train myself to unplug and disconnect, the happier I am.

Fundamental Steps

- Be in sync
- Mind your business
- Explore nature

Complete the affirmation and pay it forward by sharing with loved ones and posting on social media with a selfie.

I am #MoreThanEnough because

_____
_____
_____
_____
_____
_____
_____

If not careful, it is possible to bury opportunities to develop long-term partnerships and relationships by not minding or 'tending to' your own insecurities.

STEP SEVEN:
Just Do It Now
Reflections in Geneva, Switzerland

Never in my wildest dreams would I have thought about traveling to Europe to connect with old friends and meet new ones. I could not believe I was here because it almost did not happen. It took my friend and colleague at a neighboring college a long time to convince me to go with her to Switzerland. The plane ticket was only $550 dollars and we would stay with a friend of hers. All I needed was money for food and souvenirs.

At the time, I was a young professional and just purchased my first home and needed to save as much money as possible. The timing was perfect too because our spring breaks overlapped. My friend would meet me in Geneva after I traveled to Austria and after her travels in the countryside of Switzerland. It was a 'no-brainer.' The only caveat was making sure to make my flight during a slim window of returning from leading a spring break trip with students. Luckily, my colleague and I worked that out and I said yes. It was a go!

After a day of travel, I arrived in Geneva and met my

friend at the train station. We dropped our bags at home for the short visit, a friend's home. Then, we put on our multiple layers of clothes as we went out sightseeing in Geneva, Switzerland. We could see the Swiss Alps in the view from our window. Our first stop in the courtyard was for a photo shoot. We jumped for joy and captured each other mid-air in front of a century old mini-cathedral that overlooked the Alps.

My fascination with the crisp air near the Alps grew, and I became more inquisitive about how people grew up, what brought them to Geneva, their careers, fashion… everything! I felt like a kid in a candy store. I met so many wonderful women who lived in Switzerland, but were originally from all over the continent of Africa: Senegal, Sierra Leone, Kenya, and Tanzania. I learned more about culture and the merging of cultures. I was amazed at the diversity of people, the crisp air, and the unbelievably fresh food. The music was by far the best in terms of nightlife, and everywhere you turned there was a breathtaking view. I'll never forget those moments.

More importantly, I'll never forget the courage that it took to travel by myself to a land unknown, where I didn't speak the language and was completely unaccustomed to cultural norms. It was one of the first times when I said to myself *Just Do It*, and I did. What this experience taught me was that even if you don't plan for things to happen, sometimes you have to take the leap and make the most out of as many experiences as possible.

• • • • •

While in college, a couple of friends and I had the bright idea to demolish an old dilapidated factory and to replace it with upscale apartments for college students. Fast-forward 14 years later, there are at least 300 beautiful upscale apartments nestled between UNC-Greensboro and Guilford College in Greensboro, NC, in that exact location. Bright idea number two was a travel blog. I was traveling with my travel partner when we decided that we should write a blog about every country and city we visited and document our experiences, highlighting awesome businesses, and encouraging other young professionals to jet-set. Fast-forward 10 years later, if you Google travel blog, thousands of sites will emerge. Do awesome ideas ever creep into your brain at the most random times? Those ideas can blossom into action, or someone else will take a similar idea to the *next level*. Don't make the mistake I made of not moving ideas into action.

Other ideas developed over the years and were implemented by other people: a Cook Out fast food chain off I-95 near NC/VA border, a board game featuring African American movie facts, etc. What kept me from moving forward with these ideas? Fear of the unknown, a lack of knowledge, failure to research, and inaction cost me the potential of being a millionaire. Seriously, a millionaire.

Don't allow fear of the unknown or lack of knowledge to stop you from growing a small idea into a million-dollar business. I became annoyed with seeing my great ideas put into action by others. Now, my ideas go through a three – six-month process. I hope these steps will help you grow your next idea: Celebrate the genius in you, Create a prototype, and Chew on your mistakes.

Fundamental Steps

- Celebrate the genius in you
- Create an idea-nation
- Chew on your mistakes

Celebrate The Genius In You

When faced with a new venture, a new project or a familiar challenge, you must believe that you have *More Than Enough* genius inside of you to come to a solution. Sometimes it just takes reflecting long enough to observe and to write those things down on paper. Lauren was a client who requested a Power Hour Coaching Session. After completing the session, she felt more equipped to celebrate her genius and to put her genius to work. What was this process like? Here are four major steps to complete to assist you to do the same. Follow the Social Designs S.W.A.T. Analysis.

Document Your Strengths

What are your strengths and how often do you invest in them? Imagine receiving a paycheck for the rest of your life by only doing the things you are good at doing. What would those activities be? In the book *Strengths Finder 2.0*, Tom Rath speaks of the importance of capitalizing on our strengths. Gallup scientists discovered that, "people have several times more potential for growth when they invest energy in developing their strengths instead of correcting their deficiencies." During coaching sessions with clients, we spend an ample amount of time talking about and celebrating areas of strength. I've found that this approach not only feels better than discussing weaknesses, it also reinforces the talents and gifts of people, which in turn produces positive results.

What are your areas of strength? What are your natural talents?

_____
_____
_____
_____
_____
_____
_____
_____

List Your Wildest Dreams

Have a conversation with yourself about your wildest dreams, then write those dreams down. Lauren was a CEO at a national training center. One of her wildest dreams was to increase the minimum wage at the company by $10.00. She wanted to guarantee great salaries and part-time pay for her employees. She wrote it down and began researching and creating strategies for her dream. Within, two years, she made her dream a reality. The key factor in making her dream a reality was writing it down on paper and then putting an expiration date on it.

List your wildest dreams.

_____
_____
_____
_____
_____
_____
_____

Choose one wild dream and develop a timeline of actualization.

_____
_____
_____
_____
_____
_____
_____
_____

Understand Your Areas of Improvement

Areas of improvement are not always about improving things you suck at doing. Seek to improve your strengths too. Lauren loved her natural talent of connecting people and building relationships. However, as the CEO, she found herself in endless meetings and delegating tasks constantly. She made a huge decision to do two things. She cleared her schedule for two entire days per week for open office hours and for visiting the various departments. In this time, she deepened relationships and gained insight from employees about her goal to raise the minimum wage by $10.00.

In what ways can you improve your strengths?

_____
_____
_____
_____
_____
_____
_____
_____

Seek Training

In addition to creating more time to connect with people, Lauren also enrolled in a 6-month leadership and diversity training program and executive coaching with me. Even though she celebrated her genius, she understood the power of continual learning and training. Her skills were sharpened in the areas of active listening, conflict resolution, and communication. She also gained a better contextual understanding of the socio-economic perspectives of her employees because of the diversity training.

What types of coaching, training, or certification programs can you enroll in to sharpen your talents and gifts?

_____
_____
_____
_____
_____
_____
_____
_____

Create An Idea-Nation

Once you have an idea developed, find a way to get the idea to the world in increments. Create an "Idea-Nation." An Idea-Nation is an environment that you create that will help you to be bold and courageous. Do you have outstanding and amazing ideas that the world is waiting for? If you do not share your ideas, or write them down, or grow your ideas, they may be motionless. Whenever I have a big idea, I create a notebook just for that idea and brainstorm as many details as possible along with multiple scenarios of how to make the idea come to life. This brainstorm should also include researching the feasibility of the idea.

Write down one idea and then brainstorm as many details as possible.

_____

_____

_____

_____

_____

_____

_____

_____

_____

_____

Next share the idea with trusted friends, family, and colleagues. Communicating your idea repeatedly helps you to articulate better. You will also receive valuable feedback that you may have never thought about. Make sure you are clear with them about what type of feedback you need. Do you need a response to a specific part of your idea or do you need overall impressions?

How will you seek feedback? What specific questions will you ask?

_____
_____
_____
_____
_____
_____
_____
_____
_____
_____

Lastly, share the idea with specific industry leaders who can share wisdom and guidance about the types of business models you should follow. Most ideas require financial backing to fully flourish. Develop a budget and decide if you will raise the capital or seek investors. Once you have a plan in place, launch the idea. Take careful inventory to evaluate the process and the feedback to ensure you are measuring the return on your investment. Remember, you have what it takes. Just Do It!

Chew On Your Mistakes

    I'm tired of living in a world where people are punished when making mistakes. Imagine what life would be like if we embraced mistakes rather than ostracizing people for making them. I'm not saying we should welcome repeating mistakes. To do the same thing repeatedly to reap the same or no results is insanity. When I began to embrace mistakes as a tool for learning, I began to grow. There was pain and tears cried along the way, but life is about evolution. If I am not growing, I feel obsolete and ineffective. If things were perfect all the time, then I would not experience progress and I would stay in a stagnant state of boredom.

    Dr. Oz states, "I never regret mistakes, I regret things I never tried." Even as life is within his fingertips, he recognizes that even in the field of medicine where mistakes are taboo, it is imperative for the medical industry and doctors to evolve so that the world of medicine will be enhanced for generations to come. Yes, you risk losing, or in his case you risk life. There is always loss in making mistakes, and there is always gain. Chew on your mistakes, savor the lessons, and digest as much learning as possible.

    When I started to learn how to embrace failure, I gained a better appreciation for life. Now I chew on my mistakes like a favorite dessert. This revelation is new for me. I used to 'cry over spilled milk,' complain, and sulk in mistakes. Where did that get me? I neither learned from my mistakes, nor progressed after my mistakes. This prevented me from implementing needed changes in real time. I would pick out all the things I did wrong and obsess over every detail. The more habits you develop that allow you to be stagnant, the more stagnant you will be.

Experience taught me that failure must be a driving catalyst and not some kind of worthless reason to give up. Instead, I should have done three things to lead me on a path towards evolution and growth; **1: Recount the positive, 2: Re-envision the negative, and 3: Ask "Now What?"**

When you recount the positive, you are taking notes of everything that worked well with a project, program, or initiative. When you re-envision the negative impact, you are training your brain to troubleshoot and you are sharpening your critical thinking skills. It is easy to walk away from a failed project and say, "whelp, that's over and I'm ready to move on to the next thing." It is hard to take the time to document all your mistakes and then recreate different scenarios simply for the sake of your learning.

Asking "Now What?" takes your growing to another level. There is always a way to multiply and grow your effort for larger impact. There is always a way. The challenge is stepping up to the challenge of strategically chewing on your mistake for the long haul. Am I asking you to sit and dwell on a past project for years and years later? No. I am simply stating that in the future this project will come back around for your benefit. How different would your life be if you learned to embrace the concept of chewing on your mistakes?

Name at least one mistake in your life from which it was difficult for you to bounce back.

_____
_____
_____
_____
_____
_____
_____
_____
_____

Next, *recount the positive* ...

_____
_____
_____
_____
_____
_____
_____
_____

Then, *re-envision the negative ...*

_____
_____
_____
_____
_____
_____

Finally, ask "Now What?"

_____
_____
_____
_____
_____
_____

Fundamental Steps
- Celebrate the genius in you
- Create an idea-nation
- Chew on your mistakes

Complete the affirmation and pay it forward by sharing with loved ones and posting on social media with a selfie.

I am #MoreThanEnough because

_____

_____

_____

_____

_____

Failure must be a driving catalyst not some kind of worthless reason to give up.

STEP EIGHT:
Compete with Your Yesterday
Reflections in Saint Lucia

Banana trees
Rows and rows of huge green leaves to hold me
Mountains winding in and out of hills
Crests of clear ocean kissing soft volcanic beaches
Saint Lucia taught me to breathe
Remnants of the 70s in tunes
Stares and scolds to the foreign melanin
Saint Lucia glared back my distinctiveness
Palm trees peaking
Danger lurking
Pools on cliffs
Saint Lucia disclosed limits
Breathtaking views
Smiles inviting
Forgiveness and boundaries live on
In Saint Lucia,
I saw myself more
I led myself more
I watched myself grow for me
Saint Lucia glared back my distinctiveness
Where mountains meet oceans
Where dreams meet reality

> I thought high like Mount Gimie
> I thought long ago like Arawak
> Saint Lucy no more, here lies Lucia
> The old me no more, here lies better
> The past rich and complicated
> The future richer and complex
> I saw myself more
> I led myself more
> I watched myself grow for me
> Saint Lucia glared back my distinctiveness

Traveling to St. Lucia helped me celebrate my uniqueness. I was captivated by the cultural complexity and beauty of the island. During the time of the visit, I was faced with very tough personal and professional decisions. Will I have the courage to discontinue traditional ways of thinking or remain trapped in old customs? Should I nurture the business to reflect other business models in the industry, or should I stand out and build it my way? Just as St. Lucia did not compete with other windward islands, I didn't need to compete with anyone else. In St. Lucia, I saw myself in a distinctive light and understood myself more.

• • • • •

When I started comparing myself to my past, I was more focused and my spirit felt purer. Because no one else was in my purview, I focused on goals and strategized how to grow every single day. When you compare yourself to your yesterday you will keep a steadfast focus on your goals, not other people. Stop competing with other people. Avoid the urge to figure out if you are doing better or worse than someone else. Tell yourself regularly that you are *More Than Enough*. Craft your own path to success by creating your own lane, filtering feedback, working smarter and harder, and by leading with boldness.

Fundamental Steps

- Create your own lane
- Filter the feedback
- Work smarter and harder
- Lead with boldness

Create Your Own Lane

When I created Social Designs, a leadership and diversity company, I researched many models and best practices. I felt like I needed to be like other diversity firms for the business to grow. Over a 10-year period, and after lots of trial and error, I've learned that the Social Designs model is unique. We are different from other diversity companies because we capitalize on the process of reciprocal learning of participants using four C's: Care, Confidence, Competence, and Community. Our clients and participants are also challenged to lead with our principles of social justice: historic truth-telling, relationship building, and creative action. If I would have continued the path of comparing myself to others, the company would not be as successful as it is today. In creating my own lane, I see a huge difference in business inquiries and client development. People are spreading the word about how our services are unique, savvy, and efficient.

Create your own path of success by first understanding your passions, gifts, and talents. How do you begin this process? Think about what you are passionate about and write down three things that you would do for a living if money were not an issue.

What are you passionate about? List three things and why you are passionate about them.

_____

_____

_____

_____

_____

_____

_____

Creating your own lane means that you are developing a career and passion path that makes you happy. Think about being bold and unafraid of innovation and change. You are *More Than Enough* and you are equipped with skills gained from each chapter of your life. Those skills will prepare you to change your industry or create a totally different avenue for yourself.

An extremely talented director, writer, and entrepreneur

whose dream was to be a lawyer fighting for racial and social equality decided to create her own lane. In an interview with *Makers*, Ava DuVernay shared that,

"Women have to make movies and we don't need institutions to do that. And I think the more we can empower ourselves and know that there are other ways, that we don't have to be authenticated by the structures; that we don't have to be told that it's valid; that we find ways to make it happen, is how it changes."

Ms. DuVernay began her career as an aspiring lawyer, but later became a sought-after publicist who then realized that she wanted to and had the talent to direct. She shot her first film, *I Will Follow* in only 14 days by investing $50,000 of her savings. Ava's talent is unsurmountable with theatrical and cultural gems like the movie *Selma*, the documentary *13th*, and the television series *Queen Sugar*, which employs an entirely female staff of directors. Ava keeps getting better because she competes with her yesterday by creating her own lane.

Filter The Feedback

It was a journey for me to figure out that there are multiple lanes of success and that I am not defined by what others think of me. Sometimes people will base their feedback on assumptions they have about you and their own insecurities, instead of genuinely sharing constructive criticism.

When I think back to my earlier years, things were completely different. I think the younger I was the more I looked for the approval of others. Whether it was a friend, a boyfriend, a parent, family members, or colleagues, the approval of others was extremely important to me. That behavior had to stop. I woke up and realized that the life I have is mine to live, and no one can live it for me. Receiving advice and wisdom from other people is essential for growth, but it is of vital importance to learn how to filter the feedback you receive.

Some feedback is essential to your growth and some feedback is simply bad for your growth. However, there are lessons in the feedback you deem as bad. Find and recognize those lessons and be careful 'not to throw the baby out with the bathwater.' After writing my first book, I asked a few of people whom I respect greatly to offer feedback. There were two people who told me the book was not ready and I needed to mature more as a writer. For a moment, I took this as a sign that I was not good enough as an author. It took me about three days to bounce back from the negative feedback. I use the word negative and not constructive because neither next steps nor suggestions to make the text better were offered. Just simply the comment that I was not ready.

I was a mess! But eventually, I snapped out of it with the help of people who were pushing me to stay the course. I knew deep down that *Revolutionize Now* was timely and that it needed to happen as soon as possible. The first book I wrote is being used as curricula in middle schools, high schools, and universities in the US and Canada. Every month someone sends me a message, tells me in person, or posts on social media about the positive impact the book has had in their life. What if I would have waited? What if I would have continued to think that there was not enough evidence for my theory, or not enough personal excerpts, or not enough tips? Thousands of people would not have experienced the opportunity to learn from my experiences and strategies for social change.

Name a time in your life when you were faced with having to filter the feedback. What did you learn in the process?

_____
_____
_____
_____
_____
_____
_____
_____

Work Smarter And Harder

People often say that you should work smarter, not harder. I say that you should work smarter *and* harder. Only you know how much time and effort you are investing in your goals. When you believe that you are *more than enough*, you will do any and everything possible to reach your goals. Working smarter means that you develop habits in life that produce more efficient results. I knew that I wanted to flourish more in all areas of my life, so my strategy became sharper.

Everything in my life needed to be analyzed in a different way so that I could be as effective as possible and to do this, I needed to change habits. I changed the ways I shopped for groceries, organized my closet, pantry, and office spaces, kept records for clients, and my workout schedule to name a few things. Within weeks, I noticed clarity of thought due to my space being more practical. I discovered methods of automation for everything possible; bills, posts, and reminders. I even put out a call for interns to work with Social Designs. After learning from past trial and error with interns, I implemented new training methods that were better and yielded tremendous results.

What habits can you change or develop to create more efficiency in your life?

_____
_____
_____
_____
_____
_____

Just because I was working smarter didn't mean that I worked less. In competing with my yesterday and fully internalizing my goals and a vision for my life, the work did not decrease. However, I learned how to balance grace and 'grit' better. I'm a very hard-working woman and sometimes I don't take care of myself as much as I need to, nor do I allow much room for error. I'm a performer and thrive off results. Instead of trying to change things that are central to me, like helping others and being involved with multiple projects all at once, I celebrate my attributes. The celebration is the grace, the calm, and the voice inside that says "You can do everything perfectly. Celebrate every success whether small or large." Grace is also giving myself room to mess up and to be ok with making mistakes. The largest learning curves happen when I'm bouncing back from a mistake. I will not, however, allow the grace to stop my fierce and strong will to have grit in everything I do. Find the balance between grace and grit when working smarter and harder.

How can you balance the grace and grit in your personal and professional life?

_____

_____

_____

_____

_____

_____

_____

Lead With Boldness

Working smarter helps you to tackle obstacles head on because you are more prepared. You are more equipped to predict the unpredictable. Ask yourself, "How bad do I want it?" Yes, you can say out loud that you are *More Than Enough*, but if you are not making the necessary steps to get there, you are feeding yourself a lie. Be truthful to yourself. No one knows you better than *you*. Stop making excuses for why you are less than. Stop making excuses about what gets in the way or the societal stacks against you. Stop feeling pitiful and stop trying to gain pity support from friends and the people around you. It is time to be *More Than Enough*. It is time to lead with boldness.

I understand that circumstances may get in the way of your progress. Don't allow detours or roadblocks to dictate your destiny. You have control of what you can and will accomplish. How can you grab control of your destiny even in the face of controversy? Don't be afraid to be great. Step out of fantasizing and step into action by tackling your goals and your obstacles head-on.

How can you tackle your obstacles head-on?

_____

_____

_____

_____

Who knows where life will take us or where we will take life? The more you understand the power of believing that you are *More Than Enough*, the more you can experience what life has to offer. There is no competition because no one can be you. The *More Than Enough* belief transforms into momentum that then transitions into action because it is all about you. Make sure your actions are preceded by anticipating the unpredictable. How can you foresee what is to come? You do this by studying yourself, studying those around you, and gaining a global perspective of things that are in your purview and recognizing what's missing.

Fundamental Steps

- Create your own lane
- Filter the feedback
- Work smarter and harder
- Lead with boldness

Complete the affirmation and pay it forward by sharing with loved ones and posting on social media with a selfie.

I am #MoreThanEnough because

_____

_____

_____

_____

Don't allow detours or roadblocks to dictate your destiny.

STEP NINE:

Thrive

Reflections in Nigeria

*I*n Ebem, Ohafia, Nigeria, legend has it that if you drink from the spring where the water flows from one single rock that you have been touched directly by God's purity. Ikechukwu, my best friend Bevelyn's then fiancé, led the two of us and two of his younger cousins on a three-mile hike through the beautiful countryside. I was blown away by the sights of sandy brown and hunter green brush, thousands of trees, and the coolest tan and orange walkway of hard clay engulfing us in 10-foot-high walls.

We journeyed up and down hills and over streams to reach our destination. The hike was physically taxing, but it was worth it! The spring was an amazing sight to see! The gushing of cool and fresh water rushed from below a single rock. The current was so elegant, yet so strong. I believed the legend and drank straight from the spring. The water was so pure, so refreshing, so crisp and so quenching. After drinking the water, we found a nearby stream and swam to the middle to sit on huge smooth rocks to take in the view and sip on homemade palm wine. The serenity of nature and the intensity of our time together will forever be etched in my memory.

I remember staring into the sky and feeling like God was breathing on me. I believe in God's purity, love, joy, and peace. I believe in miracles and in purpose. I have confidence that each of us has the propensity and duty to share love and joy, to extend peace towards one another and to truly live a thriving life.

· · · · ·

Are you living to survive or are you living to thrive? Living in survival mode means existing day to day. Survival also signifies having the endurance to bounce back from danger or hardship. While it is imperative to survive through difficult moments in life, it is equally important to thrive in as many areas of life as possible. When you are surviving, you're making life happen by any means necessary, but you are just going through the motions. There are short moments of celebration but you are in a cycle of making ends meet and getting the job done 'by the skin of your teeth.' The cycle exhausts you physically, mentally, and emotionally. Breaking the cycle begins with deciding on what you value.

Thriving is the act of prospering and flourishing. In thrive mode, you work hard, break barriers (personal and societal), and you create opportunities to enjoy the fruits of your labor. Like the time we visited the spring, I want my life to be filled with ongoing moments of absolute happiness. I believe I can thrive because I'm *more than enough*. Is thriving possible all the time? I'm realizing that there are some areas where I thrive and others where I survive, and that's ok. Having a thriving mindset is challenging me to be more solution-oriented and to believe that the best of everything is available for everyone.

Computer scientist and application developer Carlos Baptista, co-created an app to track land mines to direct people away from debilitating and deadly explosions in Columbia. When he heard about the problem he told himself that he had two options, "Get used to it or try to change it with all my heart." The same attitude applies when deciding if you will continue to survive or thrive. 'Thrivers' understand that it takes practice to make flourishing a constant reality in their lives. We have multiple transitioning portions of our lives from survival mode to thriving mode. No matter if you are born with financial or social privilege or not; how you frame your mind dictates your ability to thrive. People who thrive reflect regularly, think about the meaning of life, and understand what brings them a sense of fulfillment. When you have a thriving mentality, you are seeking to create a better and healthier life. Maintaining this kind of philosophy means seeking joy, practicing discipline, staying in the lab, reinventing yourself, and remembering to balance grace and 'grit'.

Fundamental Steps

- Find joy
- Stay in the lab
- Practice discipline
- Reinvent yourself

Find Joy

2016 was an emotionally taxing year for me. It seemed like every time I turned on the television, there was a new tragedy in our country or the world. As a diversity trainer and coach, I was contracted to co-create solutions to help people respond to the tragedies of unarmed Black Americans being murdered by police officers, an increased amount of hate speech towards Jewish Americans, the mass shooting at a Gay night club, and Islamophobia. My mind and spirit was exhausted. I stopped watching the news and disconnected from social media as much as I could because I felt joy escaping me.

The issues continued and I continued to work with people to find solutions. However, to keep my spirits high and joy a constant, I decided to concentrate on what brought me pure joy. I find joy in myself because I'm worth it. I'm worth taking extended vacations or staycations. I'm worth pampering myself once a month at the spa and good quality, fresh food. I'm worth taking a 30-minute break out of my day just to take a walk in the park, binge-watching episodes of '*A Different World*' or having the Disney Movie *Moana* on repeat. I find joy talking to my mom and finding small ways to spoil her.

Imagine you are worth it. Whatever your "it" is, you are worth it. What brings you joy and happiness? How can you add you more joy into your life?

_____

_____

_____

_____

_____

_____

_____

_____

During that year I also recounted the things that did not bring me joy and I dismissed those things out of my life. Even though trying to find solutions to problems in the world decreased my joy, I decided to develop a curriculum that would aid people in a proactive manner by creating environments, policies, practices, and training programs that would lessen the probability for issues of inequality. I turned a joy-killer into a joy-creator. I took note of other things that made me unhappy, like people who complained all the time, clutter, and being out of shape. Next, I made the necessary steps to change, which included spending less time with those people, organizing my space, and working out more. I wanted and needed to assess my "normal" to step into the *next level* of thriving.

What are the things that cause negativity in your life? How can you build a life with more joy and less negativity?

_____

_____

_____

_____

_____

_____

_____

Stay In The Lab

While attending a Change-Makers conference, I was fortunate to have dinner with my childhood friend Shaneka Bynum and two other changemakers, Tim Lampkin and Akilah Watkins-Butler. I asked the following question to the group, "How can you thrive and not just survive in life?" Akilah's answer blew us all away. She advised us to "stay in the lab:" to make it a habit to do your research and over-prepare, even if there are societal stakes against you like the -isms (racism, sexism, heterosexism, classism, lookism, etc.) or poverty. Work against it, until you find a solution. Don't be afraid to break barriers, striving for success, and becoming powerful against adversity. After you break through, "stay in the lab." That is where I am now. I have been studying my craft more and I've been seeing exponential results from putting in the necessary time to grow.

Measuring growth requires a high level of focus, reflection, and documentation. Each day teaches us something, but intentionally staying in the lab prevents mistakes. Stagnation fuels and perpetuates the mentality of mere survival, but in life it's essential to keep pushing ourselves. If we are not continuously pushing ourselves, how can we get out of that mindset and really think about thriving? We can't, because we are not challenging ourselves to do better. Thriving will not come automatically. Always practice and put in the work.

How can you sharpen your skills? What do you need to study so you can elevate to a thriving lifestyle?

_____
_____
_____
_____
_____
_____

Practice Discipline

It's ironic that daily routines or habits I have are sometimes the source of my unhappiness. For example, my family brings me so much joy, especially my nieces and nephews. When I'm not around them after a long time, I'm extremely sad. However, the career I chose (which also makes me happy) does not allow as much time with them as I would like because of my demanding schedule. Sometimes we live in contradictions that get in the way of thriving. Creating harmony among those contradictions takes focused goal setting, working tirelessly, and giving up something to get the long-term reward.

What contradictions exist in your life that get in the way of thriving? What are your long-term goals? What actions are you taking to accomplish those goals? What do you need to give up to receive the reward?

_____

_____

_____

_____

_____

It takes discipline, sacrifice, and focus to get to the place of consistent long-term joy. I'm faced with choices that give me instant or delayed gratification, like deciding between spending weekends to 'cut up' with family or sacrificing that time to build a legacy for them. I experience guilt, sadness, and feel like I'm not doing enough for them, but I realize the importance of 'staying the course.' I will be unhappy if I do not see my family, yet there is a balance, and other ways to connect like phone calls, texting, FaceTime, and finding special gifts and postcards while traveling for work. Ultimately, the question I ask myself is, "What is your finish line?" This helps me to push emotions aside and to keep going. My finish line includes more flexibility with time and being a catalyst for generational growth in my family. After years of discipline, sacrifice and hard work, I'm getting closer to this reality.

What is your finish line? How are you practicing discipline to get there?

_____

_____

_____

_____

_____

_____

_____

Generational growth in education and wealth are important to me. In seeking a thriving lifestyle, discipline comes in the form of saving money and investing in education for me. Research shows that the more education you have the more likely you are to be exposed to better healthcare and the more opportunities to build wealth. Therefore, it is important for me to invest in opportunities for formal and informal education. Additionally, I have a very strict savings, and debt-payoff plan in place. These strategies are not meant for me to get rich and splurge. No, planning toward a thriving lifestyle includes putting things in place to eliminate stressors and to also invest in long-term benefits for generations to come.

How are you investing in your future?

_____

_____

_____

_____

_____

Paying school loans and saving money isn't always fun, so I found a way to make obligations exciting. For example, I love to travel and I enjoy wearing fancy clothes. People comment all the time about my perceived fabulous lifestyle and with that, assumptions arise. The unknown facts are 1: My job requires me to travel 95% of the time and 2: I'm a thrifty and creative fashionista. 50% of my clothes are from thrift stores, 20% are at least 10 years old, and 30% is usually borrowed from stylists. Because I love the work that I do and love exploring new places, I am always able to incorporate some fun during my work trips. I am blessed to do this work AND make the necessary money to pay loans and save for the future. For me, practicing discipline means that I can be creative and focus on my future.

How can you invest in your future and find ways to have fun along the way?

_____

_____

_____

_____

Reinvent Yourself

In the previous chapter, you learned how to chew on your mistakes. Use your mistakes to reinvent yourself. Take inventory of who you are and what you have done in life, then move on to something more with a heightened mindset. Albert Einstein stated, "Education is not the learning of facts, but the training of the mind to think." Once you learn how to think critically and exercise your optimism muscle, you can be anything you want to be. Some of the most well-known geniuses in the world were not always geniuses. Going through their early years from the age of 20 and sometimes all the way up to the age of 50, many people didn't do what they are most known for. They reinvented themselves.

If you are a school teacher and you want to become a chef; do it. If you are a politician and now you want to be a traveler for the rest of your life or if you are a social justice educator and now you want to change your life to do something in the business world, it is okay. It is fine to reinvent yourself whenever you want. It's your life! Don't let anyone tell you what you can or cannot do. You know what your purpose is and if your purpose changes or shifts, it is okay. It's alright to reinvent yourself. A key component in the reinvention phase, is to utilize the skills and networks you've cultivated and to transfer those talents and influencers into your new phase of life. It was difficult for me to transition into a different profession, but it was imperative if I wanted to create a thriving lifestyle. During the transition, I made sure to reflect on the successes and the lessons learned as well and my skills and talents. This was helpful and made the reinvention phase a lot easier than anticipated.

What skills and talents can you transfer during your reinvention phase? Name a few challenges and lessons learned as well as celebrations from your current or previous career.

_____

_____

_____

_____

_____

_____

Thriving begins with your mindset. Do you want a thriving life? How can you progress in thriving from five minutes a day to five days a week? Challenge your normal way of thinking by constantly seeking joy, staying in the lab, practicing discipline, and reinventing yourself.

How do you recognize what thriving is for you? How can you thrive? List 3 specific things you can do weekly to thrive.

_____

_____

_____

_____

_____
_____
_____
_____

Fundamental Steps
- Find joy
- Stay in the lab
- Practice discipline
- Reinvent yourself

Complete the affirmation and pay it forward by sharing with loved ones and posting on social media with a selfie.

I am #MoreThanEnough because

_____
_____
_____
_____
_____
_____
_____

No matter if you are born with financial or social privilege or not; how you frame your mind dictates your ability to thrive.

Closing

The journey of writing this book has been very therapeutic for me, and I hope that it has helped you to think about yourself in different, more positive ways. When I decided to write this book, it was with you in mind. I wanted to share some of my own experiences to help you understand that you are not alone on your journey to *step into the next level of you*. The journey is not easy. Like me, you may start and stop and then pick back up again. As you prepare to put the things that you have gained from this book into action, there are a few closing reminders that I'd like to share with you.

In the first chapter, I encouraged you to *Ask Yourself Why*. I want you to understand the importance of realizing your own potential, even when other people are telling you what you should or should not do with your life. Remember, this is YOUR LIFE, so never allow other people's perceptions and expectations of you hinder your growth. Always strive to *own your own power*, and while you are doing that on an increasingly regular basis (because that will take time and effort), don't forget to *satisfy a need* in your community.

Remember, you are striving for balance, not perfection. There will be times when you feel the pressure to achieve perfection, whether it be at work, or in relationships. This is the time when you must have grace for yourself. Instead of beating yourself up because you haven't achieved perfection, take time to *Reflect Deeply*. Put those fundamental steps into action! Take a time out, practice mindfulness, conquer your inconsistencies and seek knowledge. You will make mistakes along the way. Chew on them and keep it pushing. You got this!

At some point during each day take a moment to say aloud, "**I am *More Than Enough*.**" Now you have additional tools and strategies to step into the *next level of you,* so create time in your schedule to implement these fundamental steps. You are certainly worth it. Get out of survival mode and begin to thrive!

You are ***MORE THAN ENOUGH*!**

References

Baptista, C. (June, 2017). The awful logic behind land mines- and an app that helps people avoid them. Retrieved from https://www.ted.com/talks/carlos_bautista_the_awful_logic_of_land_mines_and_an_app_that_helps_people_avoid_them

Clark, Greydon, director. 1990. *The Forbidden Dance.* Columbia Pictures.

Coates, Ta-Nehisi. (2015). *Between the World and Me.* New York: Spiegel and Grau.

Duhigg, C. (2012). *The Power of Habit: Why we do what we do in life and business.* Chicago: Random House Trade Paperbacks.

DuVernay, A. (2017). Makers Profile: Ava DuVernay. Retrieved from https://www.makers.com/ava-duvernay.

Rath, T. (2007). *Strengths finder 2.0.* New York: Gallup Press.

Smith, J. (2014). *10-Day Green Smoothie Cleanse.* New York. Simon & Schuster

Glossary

Critical race theory- Interpreting and examining the impact of race and racism across multiple systems of power and within varying organizations

Lambada- The origin of the lambada is the carimbo. Both dances come from Portuguese, African, and Indigenous cultures in Brazil.

Liberatory consciousness- Coined by Dr. Barbara Love, a belief that enables humans to live their lives in oppressive systems and institutions with awareness and intentionality, while being aware of societal norms they have been accustomed to

Social Designs- a training and development firm specializing in leadership and diversity

Youth Action Project (YAP)- annual social justice youth conference hosted and supported by the White Privilege Conference

Jada's Motivation Playlist

Live Your Life, T.I. (featuring Rihanna)

Unwritten, Natasha Bedingfield

Stronger, Kanye

Ah Feeling Mehself, Patrice Roberts

Firework, Katy Perry

Good Times, Chic

If I Could Give You, Justin The Beloved

Change, J. Cole

Button Up Flow, D. Lloyd

Sunday Morning Jetpack, Big Sean (featuring The Dream)

Phenomenal, Benjai

Clean Up, The Canton Spirituals

Keep Your Head to the Sky, Earth, Wind & Fire

Say it Loud (I'm Black & I'm Proud), James Brown

Lifting Up the Name of Jesus, Helen Baylor

Fine, Mary J. Blige

Joy & Pain, Maze

Hard, Rhianna

Love Yourz, J. Cole

Faithful, Common

Free Your Dreams, Chantae Cann

Cloud 9, Lyrikal

If I Ruled the World, Nas

Four Leaf Clover, Erykah Badu

Sassy, Rapsody

Something About the Name of Jesus, The Rance Allen Group (featuring Kirk Franklin)

Bigger Than Me, Big Sean (featuring The Flint Chozen Choir & Starrah)

Ambition, Wale

Hi Hater Remix, Maino (featuring T.I., Swizz Beats, Plies, Jadakiss, Fabolous)

Survivor, Destiny's Child

Live Like We Were Dying, Kris Allen

Keep Your Head Up, Tupac

Sky's the Limit, Notorious B.I.G.

All I Do Is Win, DJ Khaled (featuring T-Pain, Ludacris, Snoop Dogg, Rick Ross)

Fighter, Christina Aguilera

Cheers, Rihanna (featuring Jeezy)

Acknowledgements

First of all, I'm grateful to God for giving me life and the opportunity to spread this positive message of courage. Thank you to friends and family for your support and allowing me to ask you over and over again why you are *more than enough*. Thank you to my mother for teaching me to always be myself and to never allow anyone to steer me away from God's promises. I'm appreciative for such an excellent branding company to be behind this project. Thank you to the KPE Media team for the book design, photography, and media campaign. This book was written from a series of empowerment speeches and coaching strategies that began as an uplifting statement. I am grateful to those who have supported the quest of sharing *More Than Enough* as a movement. Adding the local and global travel reflections made writing this book enjoyable. Thank you, Carla Bluitt for the suggestion of capturing moments of cultural exchange on paper. You're a genius. Thank you, Holly Canada Wilson, for your encouragement and your sharp eye as the editor of *More Than Enough*. I appreciate you for constantly reminding me that I am *more than enough* throughout this process. Bevelyn Afor Ukah your attention to prose and voice has taught me so much as a writer and a thinker. Thank you for our challenging and fun-filled writing sessions. To those of you mentioned in the book, you're added depth to my life simply by allowing me to be in your presence. Shaneka Bynum, our hard conversations about thriving pushed not only my thinking, but my philosophy of life and how I approach my life's work. Thank you for your honesty and loyalty for the last 20+ years. Finally, to my special friend, I'm grateful for your encouragement and unwavering support throughout my journey of truly believing in myself and the abilities I've been blessed with. Thank you for not allowing me to settle for less than and for teaching me countless life lessons.

About the Author

Jada Monica Drew is a Leadership and Diversity Consultant who partners with organizational and educational leaders to create professional development solutions in leadership and diversity for personnel and to develop sustainable practices for equity and inclusion. After spending nearly a decade working in collegiate multicultural affairs and serving as an adjunct faculty member, Jada knows what truly drives systemic change, retention, and community partnerships- and it's not mastering a perfect calendar of events. It's building relationships, historic truth-telling, and creative action.

Jada has supported the implementation of the Diversity Plan, campus-wide Understanding Racism training, and leading the formation of the Black Alumni Advisory Board at Guilford College. She has also worked to cultivate resource groups with Leadership for Educational Equity while serving as a Director of Diversity Equity & Inclusion. In collaboration with national educators, Jada directs the international Youth Action Project (YAP) of the White Privilege Conference.

In addition to her extensive leadership and diversity experience, Jada is a certified True Colors International and a certified Intercultural Development Inventory trainer. She also serves as a co-chair of the Other Voices Greensboro Chamber of Commerce Program and is a board member of both ArtsGreensboro and American Friends Service Committee.

In her first book, *Revolutionize Now: Creative Leadership & Action for Social Change*, Jada supports readers to create a blueprint for self-discovery and social change.

Jada holds a BS in Psychology from Guilford College and a MS in Global & International Education from Drexel University. She is also recognized as a United Nations DPINGO speaker and featured in Made in Greensboro.

Stay in Touch with Jada

Subscribe to her Growth Tips at www.SocialDesignsConsulting.com to learn how to put your talents and big ideas into action.

Book Jada for executive coaching, consulting, trainings and keynotes at www.JadaMonicaDrew.com
@JadaMonicaDrew
#MoreThanEnough

All material published by Social Designs, LLC in any medium is protected by copyright. Written permission is required for any other reproduction of material by a business or independent consultant.

Requests for permission may be submitted by mail or email:

Permissions
Social Designs, LLC
PO Box 77113
Greensboro, NC 27417
socialdesignsconsulting@gmail.com

www.ingramcontent.com/pod-product-compliance
Lightning Source LLC
Chambersburg PA
CBHW070917160426
43193CB00011B/1491